"A helpful addition to the ever-expanding literature on Pope Francis. This collection will no doubt be greeted with gratitude by those desiring personal growth in their lives through reflection on the Pope's words and actions, especially his determination to build bridges, foster receptive dialogue, and multiply opportunities for encounter."

–Cardinal Pietro Parolin, Vatican Secretary of State

"This brilliant collection fizzes with the tension and tumult of this most provocative and enigmatic of papacies. Francis—the top-down decentralizer, the champion of the peripheries who draws the world's attention to the personality at the center, the blunt speaker who leaves exasperated critics desiring tidiness and clarity—has triggered a creative commotion. No one ever has ever quite captured it; McElwee and Wooden's kaleidoscope comes close."

-Brendan Walsh, editor of *The Tablet*

Key Words of Pope Francis

edited by Joshua J. McElwee and Cindy Wooden

foreword by Ecumenical Patriarch Bartholomew

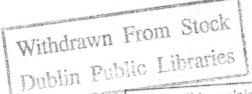
BLOOMSBURY CONTINUUM
LONDON · NEW YORK · OXFORD · NEW DELHI · SYDNEY

BLOOMSBURY CONTINUUM
Bloomsbury Publishing Plc
50 Bedford Square, London, WC1B 3DP, UK

BLOOMSBURY, BLOOMSBURY CONTINUUM and
the Diana logo are trademarks of Bloomsbury Publishing Plc

First published in 2018 in the United States of America as *A Pope Francis Lexicon*
(Liturgical Press © 2018 by Order of Saint Benedict, Collegeville, Minnesota).

First published in Great Britain 2018

Cindy Wooden and Joshua J. McElwee have asserted their rights under the Copyright,
Designs and Patents Act, 1988, to be identified as Editors of this work.

Translations by Marco Batta (Archbishop Victor Fernández), Barry Hudock
(Andrea Tornielli and Msgr. Dario Viganò), and Junno Arocho Esteves (Cardinal
Óscar Rodríguez Maradiaga).

A catalogue record for this book is available from the British Library.

ISBN: TPB: 9781472955777; ePub: 9781472955760; ePDF: 9781472955753

2 4 6 8 10 9 7 5 3 1

Typeset by Newgen Knowledge Works (P) Ltd., Chennai, India
Printed and bound in Great Britain by CPI Group (UK) Ltd, Croydon CR0 4YY

To find out more about our authors and books visit
www.bloomsbury.com and sign up for our newsletters

Contents

Foreword

Ecumenical Patriarch Bartholomew

It is with great joy that we join this delightful "anthology," a Greek word that denotes a charming selection of engaging reflections, a compilation of fragrant offerings to a prominent religious leader.

This volume is a collection of reflections on key words in the message and ministry of our beloved brother, Pope Francis. Words, however, are much more than conventional remarks; they are far more important than ordinary utterances. Words are the intrinsic expression of life, our most intimate reflection of divinity, the very identity of God: "In the beginning was the Word, and the Word was with God, and the Word was God" (John 1:1).

Indeed, we are judged by every word that comes from our lips (Matt 12:36). Words can heal or crush (Prov 12:6), prove productive or destructive (Prov 8:21), generate benevolence and edification (Eph 4:29) or else bitterness and imprecation (Rom 3:14). Most of all, we should "be ready to give an explanation to anyone who asks you for a reason for your hope" (1 Pet 3:15).

In our encounters and exchanges with our brother, the Bishop of Rome, we have experienced the profound sacredness of words. We remember and recognize that words either build bridges or build walls. Therefore, together, we have sought to promulgate a dialogue of love and a dialogue of truth, "living the truth in love" (Eph 4:15).

Of course, while words may express and describe human affections, they can never adequately exhaust or define the human heart. However, they reveal glimpses into the world of another human being; they present insights into their interests and concerns. If we pay attention to the frequency with which we repeat and accentuate particular words, we will observe the patterns and passions that shape our life.

This is why we were not surprised to see the terms selected in this volume as characteristic and suggestive of the fundamental *principles* prioritized and personalized by Pope Francis:

- his ministry is devoted to Jesus and the church as the Body of Christ, while exposing clerical abuse and encouraging accountability;
- he strives to relate the sacraments of the church to the life of the world, such as baptism to tears;
- within the church as institution, he wishes to decrease clericalism and increase collegiality, while addressing indifference and advocating discernment;
- in his church's relations with others, he promotes dialogue and ecumenism, as well as encounter and embrace;
- in the global community, he discerns the intricate connection between capitalism and creation, persecution and refugees; and
- he cares about family, women, children, and grandparents.

Above all, we were struck by the specific *virtues* that form the contours of his message and witness:

- dignity and justice,
- mercy and hope, but above all
- love and joy.

This book transcends mere words. It is a splendid mosaic of colourful, engaging elements that unveil the sympathetic and compassionate man we have come to know as Pope Francis.

From the Phanar
July 2017

Ecumenical Patriarch Bartholomew is the archbishop of Constantinople–New Rome and spiritual leader of 300 million Orthodox Christians worldwide.

Preface

Cardinal Seán O'Malley, OFM Cap

I have always liked the story about the Jesuit and the Franciscan who are walking down the street one day when suddenly they are accosted by a young man who says to them: "Fathers, can you tell me what novena I should make to acquire a BMW?" The Franciscan said: "What is a BMW?" And the Jesuit said: "What's a novena?"

We have a pope who defies these categories as he melds the Jesuit and the Franciscan into one. But I believe that Pope Francis is the quintessential Ignatian Jesuit. We have a pope who has embraced the vocation of being a follower of "Ignatius who wants to be a saint like St. Francis." Our pope is thoroughly Jesuit, thoroughly Ignatian, right down to the fascination with St. Francis. During the first year of his pontificate in an interview for *Civiltà Cattolica*, Jesuit Fr. Antonio Spadaro asked Pope Francis why he became a Jesuit. The pope said that three things about the Jesuits that attracted him were: the missionary spirit, community and discipline—including how they manage their time.

It is quite obvious that Pope Francis exhibits these characteristics in spades. He is truly living his Jesuit vocation with an intense missionary zeal, a love for community, a community for mission, and the disciplined life that does not waste anything, especially not time. Shortly before his ordination, the thirty-two-year-old Jorge Bergoglio wrote a short "credo," and he has shared that even now he keeps that document close at hand, as a reminder of his core convictions. It is a clear indication of the habit of self-reflection so deeply ingrained by his Jesuit formation.

Pope Francis embraces the introspection that is so central to Jesuit spirituality. The practice of the *examen* undertaken individually wherever and whenever the circumstances permitted was Ignatius's plan to keep the Jesuits recollected in God, to keep them focused despite their activist lifestyles. Reflecting this spiritual focus in his address to the Brazilian bishops at World Youth Day in 2013, the Holy Father asked: "Unless we train ministers capable of warming people's hearts, of walking with them in the night, of dialoguing with their hopes and disappointments, of mending their brokenness, what joy can we have for our present and future?"

Pope Francis reminds us that God's heart has a special place for the poor. He is most eloquent in his advocacy on behalf of the poor, reminding all of us of our obligation to help them by programmes of promotion and assistance, as well as by working to resolve the structural causes of poverty. In *Evangelii Gaudium* the Holy Father presents one of his most impassioned pleas on behalf of the poor by emphasizing the importance of providing them with pastoral care as he states: "I want to say with regret that the worst discrimination which the poor suffer is the lack of spiritual care. The great majority of the poor have a special openness to the faith; they need God and we must not fail to offer them His friendship, His blessing, His Word, the celebration of the sacraments and a journey of growth and maturity in the faith. Our preferential option for the poor must mainly translate into a privileged and preferential religious care" (EG 200).

Pope Francis has also shared that Catholicism is not a "catalogue of prohibitions." He urges us to be positive, to emphasize the things that unite us, not those which divide us, to prioritize the connection between people and the path we walk together, observing that after focusing on what brings us together then the work of addressing the differences becomes easier. The Holy Father also advises us that every form of catechesis should attend to the "way of beauty," showing others that to follow Christ is not only right and true but is also something beautiful, capable of filling life with new splendour and profound joy, even in the midst of difficulties.

Pope Francis understands that the words we use to speak about the people of God and the work of the church are of great importance and can often make the difference between a person being open to hearing more, to considering a life of faith; or turning away feeling rejected, dismissed or relegated as unworthy. Beginning with the spiritual reflection that all our gifts, talents and achievements are gifts from God, the Holy Father has given us a vocabulary of care, concern, inclusion and service. With the help of God and one another may we take these teachings to heart and go forward as missionary disciples for Christ.

From Boston
August 2017

Cardinal Seán O'Malley, OFM Cap, is the archbishop of Boston and a member of the Council of Cardinals.

Baptism

Cardinal Donald Wuerl

"You will be my witnesses" (Acts 1:8). This charge reflects the great evangelizing mandate that Jesus gives to his apostles and disciples. Before he ascended to heavenly glory, the risen Jesus said to his followers—and by extension to the whole church—that we were to "go and make disciples of all nations baptizing them . . . teaching them to observe all that I have commanded you" (Matt 28:19-20). How would this take place, how would we be able to achieve such a mighty task? In telling us we would be his witnesses, Jesus also assured us, "You will receive power when the holy Spirit comes upon you" (Acts 1:8).

It is precisely in the outpouring of the Holy Spirit that we are members of Christ's church and thus receive the mission to be witnesses and, at the same time, are given the power by which we will accomplish our task as evangelizing disciples. In the sacrament of baptism where all sin is washed away, the gift of the Holy Spirit is imparted and we become members of the church. "No one can enter the kingdom of God without being born of water and Spirit" (John 3:5). This connection between baptism, mission, and discipleship is present first in Sacred Scripture as told in Jesus' message but also is a cornerstone in the teaching and ministry of Pope Francis.

Three elements are at the core of our missionary discipleship: first receiving the Holy Spirit through baptism, next accepting to follow Christ, and finally being willing to share the Good News. Again and again in using the word "baptism," the Holy Father says that, in addition to receiving this gift of new life personally and rather than keeping it for ourselves, a priority in our lives is to go out and generously spread Christ's merciful love. "In virtue of their baptism, all the members of the People of God have become missionary disciples," he affirmed in his first apostolic exhortation, which followed the Synod of Bishops on the New Evangelization convened by Pope Benedict XVI, adding that "the New Evangelization calls for personal involvement on the part of each of the baptized" (*Evangelii Gaudium* 120).

In his encyclical letter *Lumen Fidei*, we learn how baptism "modifies all our relationships, our place in this world and in the universe, and opens them to God's own life of communion," as they point also to the importance of those preparing for baptism for the New Evangelization (42).

Our Holy Father encourages us, even if we do not remember being baptized, to remember the date when we received the sacrament. "To know the date of our Baptism is to know a blessed day. . . . We must reawaken the memory of our Baptism. We are called to live out our Baptism every day as the present reality of our lives. If we manage to follow Jesus and to remain in the church, despite our limitations and with our weaknesses and our sins, it is precisely in the Sacrament whereby we have become new creatures and have been clothed in Christ" (general audience, January 8, 2014).

In baptism, we learn the crucial lessons of relationship and gift, of how we are not isolated individuals living for ourselves but are all intertwined as a people who are meant to care for one another. Through baptism, we become a member of a community of evangelizing disciples—evangelizing missionaries. In his most recent apostolic exhortation, *Amoris Laetitia*, Pope Francis explains this connection, "Mutual self-giving in the sacrament of matrimony is grounded in the grace of baptism, which establishes the foundational covenant of every person with Christ in the church. In accepting each other, and with Christ's grace, the engaged couple promise each other total self-giving, faithfulness and openness to new life" (73).

Pope Francis goes on to say, "We are called to live out our baptism every day as the present reality of our lives. . . . By our baptism, we recognize in the least and in the poor the face of the Lord who visits us and makes himself close. Baptism helps us to recognize in the face of the needy, the suffering, and also of our neighbour, the face of Jesus" (general audience, January 8, 2014). Having received in the sacrament the life of Jesus and moved by his example, he explains, "we want to enter fully into the fabric of society, sharing the lives of all, listening to their concerns, helping them materially and spiritually in their needs, rejoicing with those who rejoice, weeping with those who weep; arm in arm with others, we are committed to building a new world" (EG 269).

This evangelizing task to which Pope Francis refers so insistently is the work of all of us. We are not simply bystanders watching events unfold around us. That is certainly true when we face the many challenges presented today by a secular culture, in which we are called to be the visible sign of a better and fuller way of living. Pope Francis tells us to go out, encounter, engage and accompany people as we try to share with them the story and Gospel of Jesus.

To go out is to be able to leave our comfort zone and actually reach out to those who perhaps should be with us and are not, and with whom we may have regular contact.

To encounter means to carry on our ordinary, daily life but this time aware that many of the people we meet, work and recreate with may really know very little of the values that we cherish—of the wonder of the Gospel message and of the joy that it brings.

Now comes the action of engagement. We have to be open to initiating a conversation or responding in the midst of conversations that challenge the values that we hold dear. Sometimes this can take on the form of a simple "I have another take on that" comment when you hear people talking about life, actions, values, or morality in a way that ignores Christ, his Gospel and our own appreciation of the Good News. Then it falls to us to be the witness and to have the courage to be able to say, "You know, I see things a bit differently than that."

While we see things very differently than many of the people with whom we associate, our task is not to accept what is said and done as if we have nothing to bring to the discussion. It is not just that we go out, we encounter, but we actually engage.

The call of Pope Francis is to a New Evangelization in action, beginning with baptism. He offers a renewed experience of living the Gospel. He invites us, as he did in the Jubilee of Mercy, to experience personally God's tender affection and saving love, and also to "regain the conviction that we need one another, that we have a shared responsibility for others" (*Laudato Si'* 229).

Amidst the human condition and all the modern struggles people may face, Pope Francis's engaging invitation to experience the closeness of the church, and for us disciples, baptized in the Spirit, to be caring and compassionate, strikes me as precisely the hope and grace we need today.

Cardinal Donald Wuerl is the archbishop of Washington, DC. He is a member of the Vatican's Congregations for the Doctrine of the Faith, for Bishops, and for Clergy.

Benedict XVI

David Gibson

Few domestic arrangements can prove more awkward or stressful than suddenly having to accommodate an ageing relative. Apart from the logistics of finding a suitable room and providing proper care, the pressures of such a move can create tensions between spouses and with in-laws, or revive memories of past domestic squabbles that had been buried but not resolved.

Now imagine that the ageing relative is a former pope, the Holy Father, the first pontiff to retire from the See of Peter in some six hundred years, and you have just been elected to serve as the new pope—in effect the new *paterfamilias*, head of a clan with some 1.2 billion members, many of whom are still in shock at the departure of the previous pope. Then you have some sense of the freighted scenario that greeted Pope Francis in March 2013 when he assumed the Petrine mantle from Pope Benedict XVI, now with the word "emeritus" tucked into his title.

So how did Francis seek to defuse a potentially explosive situation?

First, as he so often does, through gestures: Francis called Benedict immediately after his election on March 13, 2013, and he used Benedict's pastoral staff at his inaugural Mass in St. Peter's Square while the retired pope watched on television from Castel Gandolfo, the papal summer villa outside Rome where Benedict had secluded himself while the conclave unfolded at the Vatican. A few days later Francis went to visit Benedict for lunch and pay his respects.

Then a few weeks after that, when renovations on the Mater Ecclesiae Monastery inside the Vatican walls had been completed in order to better accommodate the retired pope, Francis was there to greet his predecessor with his characteristic warmth. The two went to the chapel to pray together, and from that point on Francis continued to honour Benedict publicly at every turn, symbolically and substantively, even as Benedict made sure everyone knew that he deferred to Francis.

Francis's first encyclical—considered a foundational document for a new pontificate—was titled *Lumen Fidei*, or "The Light of Faith," and had been started by Benedict. But rather than casting it aside to write something wholly his own, Francis used the framework and added his own thoughts and approach. He called it "the work of four hands," and made sure to invite Benedict to join him in blessing a new statue of St. Michael the Archangel in the Vatican Gardens in July 2013 on the morning the encyclical was officially released.

A short time later Francis sent Benedict a prepublication copy of his first major interview, with the Jesuit magazine *La Civiltà Cattolica*, so that Benedict could "read it and write down any criticism he may have," as Archbishop Georg Gänswein, Benedict's personal secretary, put it. Benedict "did his homework" (as the professor-pope would, of course) and sent back four pages of comments. That only cemented Benedict's reputation as what Italian Vaticanista Andrea Gagliarducci called "Pope Francis's hidden adviser."

Francis also made sure to invite Benedict to major Vatican ceremonies, such as the naming of new cardinals, and when the retired pope could come he would doff his white zucchetto, or skullcap, in a sign of respect before the two shared a fraternal embrace. When the retired pontiff was not feeling up to appearing at the consistories for new cardinals, Francis and the new cardinals would be sure to visit the emeritus pontiff. Francis even told the story that when some of his critics reportedly went to Benedict privately to complain about Francis, Benedict sent them packing.

But beyond gestures, it is above all in the words that Francis uses to refer to Benedict that you can best discern his approach to dealing with what for some would be a perplexing or problematic situation. Not so for Francis, who early on said that having Benedict living in the Vatican was like having a "wise grandfather" around.

"I have said many times that it gives me great pleasure that he lives here in the Vatican, because it is like having a wise grandfather at home," Francis said at a 2014 event attended by Benedict. He later upped the praise, calling his predecessor the "grandfather of all grandfathers."

It's an affecting formulation, yes. But it has a serious message and a concrete effect of elevating Benedict by placing him in the context of the family—the domestic reality that Francis sees as the key to the future of the church and the world. The family is, as he has said, "a factory of hope" for the church and society. Getting married and having children is not easy, he admits, and it can be difficult to have relatives of all ages hanging around the house. "Families have difficulties. Families, we quarrel, and sometimes plates can fly. And children bring headaches," as Francis told the World Meeting of Families in Philadelphia in September 2015. "But in families there is always light, because the love of God, and Son of God, opened also that path for us."

The elderly are especially prized family members to Francis, and that's not simply a principle with the pope; it's also personal. His grandmother, Rosa, was a great influence on young Jorge Mario Bergoglio when he grew up in the Argentine capital of Buenos Aires, and he still keeps a note from her written to him on the day of his ordination as a priest in his breviary.

Of course it can be a bit amusing to read about a pope who's over eighty referring to a pope emeritus who just turned ninety as his grandfather. But Francis is also including himself in this framing, viewing senior citizens like him and Benedict in a biblical perspective that provides the fundamental grounding for his views of his predecessor.

For example, Francis often cites the passage in Luke when the aged Simeon, a righteous old man waiting for death, came to the Temple and with joy recognized the infant Jesus as the Messiah; and Anna, an eighty-four-year-old widow who was revered as a prophet also recognized Jesus as the Messiah. He also likes to cite the example of Abraham, as he did in June 2017 in a homily for the twenty-fifth anniversary of his own ordination as a bishop.

Speaking to other bishops in attendance, Francis noted that Abraham was seventy-five years old when God told him to leave his country with his family and possessions to go and start a new nation in a new land. "He was more or less our age," Francis said. "He was about to retire, to retire to rest. . . . He started out at that age. An elderly man, with the weight of old age, that old age that brings pains, sicknesses." Yet God sent him out "as if he were a scout."

The pope noted that some church critics mock the hierarchy as "the gerontocracy of the church."

But no, Francis insists. Like Simeon and Anna and Abraham, he said, "we are grandfathers called to dream and to give our dream to today's youth: they need it, because they will draw from our dreams the strength to prophesy and to carry their task forward."

For Francis, grandfathers like Benedict—like he himself, and all seniors—are rooted in our past but they are hardly history. They live in the present, and they are, as Oscar Romero would put it, prophets of a future not their own.

David Gibson is director of Fordham University's Center on Religion and Culture. He is a veteran journalist who has covered the Vatican since the 1980s and is the author of The Rule of Benedict: Pope Benedict XVI and His Battle with the Modern World.

Capitalism

Bishop Robert McElroy

Pope Francis has at times excoriated the logic of the capitalist system as "the dung of the devil," a "subtle dictatorship," and a "new form of colonialism." At other moments the pope has pointed to the achievements of market economies in alleviating global poverty through creativity and freedom, applauding in his address before the US Congress in September 2015 "the right use of natural resources, the proper application of technology and the harnessing of the spirit of enterprise [that] are essential elements of an economy which seeks to be modern, inclusive and sustainable."

Francis shares the conviction of St. John Paul II in *Centesimus Annus* that the substantial creativity and freedom inherent in market economies must be "circumscribed within a strong juridical framework which places [them] at the service of human freedom in its totality, and which sees it as a particular aspect of that freedom, the core of which is ethical and religious" (CA 42).

But while the experience of John Paul in the statist dictatorship of Eastern Europe after World War II led him to underscore the ways in which government control threatens the freedom of the human person in economic and social life, Pope Francis brings the perspective of the Global South to bear, revealing that free markets can generate a totalitarian ethos no less dangerous to the common good and the dignity of the human person. For this reason, the preferential option for the poor becomes for Pope Francis the fundamental prism through which to evaluate capitalism and free market systems. It is through the eyes and the experience of those who are poorest among us that we must judge the moral legitimacy of every economic system and discern the nature of the juridical circum-scription that is necessary to promote a just economic order.

In carrying out this evaluation, Pope Francis emphasizes that it is capitalism in the concrete, not as a philosophical system, that must be scrutinized. There is a sense of deep urgency to Francis's discussion of the need to reform radically the market system of the current global economy, an urgency that flows from his experiences on the streets of Buenos Aires, his visits to Bolivia, Sri Lanka and the Central African Republic, and his encounters with the continuing tragedies of the world's refugee crisis. The question of capitalism is for the pope not a matter of speculative debate among competing abstract systems, but the moral imperative to recognize amidst the creative capacity of the current global economy the presence of destructive patterns that destroy lives, physically, spiritually, and morally. This economy kills!

The first destructive pattern of twenty-first-century global capitalism is the strangling force of inequality that it breeds in the world. As Pope Francis wrote in *Evangelii Gaudium*, "The need to resolve the structural causes of poverty cannot be delayed. . . . As long as the problems of the poor are not radically resolved by rejecting the absolute autonomy of markets and financial speculation and by attacking the structural causes of inequality, no solution will be found for the world's problems, or, for that matter, to any problems. Inequality is the root of social ills" (EG 202).

Francis identifies this inequality as the foundation for a process of exclusion that cuts immense segments of society off from meaningful participation in social, political, and economic life. It gives rise to a fi-nancial system that rules rather than serves humanity and a capitalism that discards those who have no utility as consumers. The Second Vatican Council condemned grave economic inequality, as "a source of scandal [that] militates against social justice, equity, human dignity, as well as social and international peace" (*Gaudium et Spes* 29). And each of the modern popes has identified the multi-dimensional harm of grave in-equality that is destructive on material, cultural, and spiritual levels. But in the concept of exclusion, Pope Francis has captured the devastation wrought by global capitalism and its capacity to effectively annihilate human identity in society.

If direct destruction to human lives and the human community consti-tute the central failing of the global economy of our day, the destruction to the world that is our common home constitutes a second, powerfully devastating consequence of capitalist structures, according to Francis. The logic of market systems that privatize profits while placing the environmental destruction wrought by such profits in the public sphere has contributed enormously to the cascade of destruction that is suffocating the earth.

Commenting on the manner in which the very structures and moral claims of the free-market system threaten the earth, Pope Francis sorrowfully observes: "Whatever is fragile, like the environment, is defenceless before the interests of a deified market, which becomes the only rule" (EG 56). And the structures of inequality endemic to capitalist economies accentuate the disproportionate devastation of the poor which takes place through environmental degradation, resulting in the inversion of the preferential option: the poor always suffer the first and most intense effects of environmental damage.

The final central defect that Pope Francis identifies in the global capitalism of the present day is a spiritual one. In its twin foundations of the ever greater accumulation of material possessions and economic power, capitalism is inherently spiritually corrosive. The driving force of a capitalist system is the desire to accumulate. It is not rooted in the drive to create, to benefit society, or to build culture, but in the need to acquire. Such an economic system makes it ever more difficult to build a culture that is not trapped in materialism and the drive to dominate.

Pope Francis speaks often of the "deification" of the current global market system. In this concept he provides a perspective for strengthening the creativity and freedom that form the positive contributions of capitalist systems, while also addressing with a sense of urgency the three threats of structural inequality, market-driven devastation of the environment, and the danger of spiritual corrosion that are intermeshed with market systems. Only when it is recognized that free markets are not a first principle of economic justice, but merely a means to achieve such justice, can the construction of an effective and balanced juridical order within and among nations realistically advance.

Bishop Robert McElroy leads the Diocese of San Diego, California. He has doctorates in theology and political science and serves on the US bishops' administrative, ecumenical, domestic justice, and international affairs committees.

Careerism

Cardinal Joseph W. Tobin, CSsR

Careerism among ordained ministers in the church is both an attitude and a behaviour that Pope Francis has denounced frequently, often with blunt language and colourful images. This public stance carries some degree of risk, since he often challenges his closest collaborators—cardinals, bishops, officials in the Roman Curia, and priests in the diplomatic service of the Holy See, as well as rank-and-file pastors across the globe. Some bishops complain that such rhetoric discourages them and their priests. In fact, a papal spokesman characterized Francis as an "anti-clerical pope," given his suspicion of the propensity to power and privilege that is often associated with the church's clerics.

How does Pope Francis understand careerism? What provokes his harsh condemnation? What sort of remedy does he suggest?

For Francis, careerism is an understanding of one's position in the church in terms of what one can obtain, rather than what one can give. It is an attitude as ancient as the question of the mother of James and John (Matt 20:20-23) or the dispute among the apostles over who of them was the greatest (Luke 22:24-30). In the view of Francis, clerical pursuit of advancement, power, and prestige harms the church in a number of ways. Careerism guts the reality of ordained ministry as a vocation—that is, a specific way of life to which God calls some to live their baptismal commitment. Instead of a life of discipleship—a life that is essentially a response to the invitation of the Master who "did not come to be served but to serve and to give his life as a ransom for many" (Mark 10:45)—

the ambitious cleric pursues his own venal designs. God has not chosen him; rather, he has chosen an ecclesiastical career for the privileges that it promises him.

Careerism produces collateral damage among the cleric's peers and colleagues. Francis underscores the harm done by gossip, rivalries, and polarizing divisions among priests and bishops. A shrewd cleric will view pastoral service and personal opinions according to their potential for advancing him in church structure, while remaining indifferent or cold to people or situations that do not promise some return on his efforts. Such calculations are difficult to conjugate with the figure of the Good Shepherd, who "lays down his life for the sheep" (John 10:11).

It is helpful to recall that Pope Francis has been a member of the Society of Jesus for nearly six decades and one may assume that the spirituality of the Jesuits continues to influence him. That spirituality recommends attention to the deepest desires of one's heart, since desire is a primary way that God leads people to discover who they are and what they are meant to do. The search for fulfilment through the acquisition of titles, prestige or power can insulate a priest or bishop from confronting the real desires of his heart and lead him to the tragedy of "gain[ing] the whole world and forfeit[ing] his life" (Mark 8:36).

In fact, what may strike some listeners as simply a harsh screed against clerical ambition might offer another connection to Jesuit spirituality, an invitation to the practice of *particular examen*. Far from tarring all ordained ministers with the same brush, the Holy Father asks clerics to find the movement of God in all the people and events of daily life. An honest examination of one's real motivations against the example of the Master may be an invitation to conversion.

The force and frequency of his criticism manifest the high esteem of Francis for the pastoral service of priests and bishops. He is not calling for a sort of levelling movement that would eliminate ordained ministry in the church. Episcopal office, for example, should not be sought, requested, bought or sold, but embraced in obedience. At the same time, there is great beauty in the office of bishop and communion with him is essential for the spiritual health of the people. The true glory of these ministries comes from the opportunities they offer to lay down one's life for others. Nevertheless, as Francis reminded students at the Pontifical Ecclesiastical Academy, the Roman faculty that prepares future diplomats for the Holy

See, "all types of priestly ministry require great inner freedom," which calls for "vigilance in order to be free from ambition or personal aims, which can cause so much harm to the church" (June 6, 2013).

In that same address, he called careerism a form of "leprosy" among ordained ministers: "Careerism is a leprosy, a leprosy. . . . Please, no more careerism!" Leprosy is known as a disfiguring disease that traditionally has isolated its victims from the community. For Pope Francis, careerism distorts the beauty of the vocation of priests and bishops and will ruin their relation with the people they are called to serve. The people become instruments for the minister's self-aggrandizement (cf. Ezek 34:2), and finally they will flee self-serving leaders (John 10:8, 10).

Pope Francis has taken some practical steps to reduce the temptations to careerism among the ordained. First, he insists that seminaries promote a model of ministry that adheres closely to the example of Christ, the poor, lowly, and generous servant of humankind. He has restricted the bestowal of titles like "monsignor" and uncoupled the nomination of cardinals from traditional sees. By spurning pomp and privilege in favour of simplicity and generosity, Pope Francis provides personal witness to Jesus, the Good Shepherd.

Cardinal Joseph Tobin is the archbishop of Newark, New Jersey. He previously served as the archbishop of Indianapolis from 2012 to 2016, as the secretary of the Vatican's Congregation for Institutes of Consecrated Life and Societies of Apostolic Life from 2010 to 2012, and as the superior general of the Redemptorists from 1997 to 2009.

Church

Elizabeth Stoker Bruenig

"*Mater si, magistra no,*" (mother yes, teacher no) may have begun life as an expression of conservative revolt against Pope John XXIII's 1961 encyclical *Mater et Magistra* (mother and teacher), but the phrase has since become shorthand for any brand of Catholic who appreciates the emotional benefits of the church but ignores her teaching.

That such a slogan ever needed to be coined is troubling enough. But the statement itself also presents a rather limited view of what it is that mothers do. If appointing the church as mother makes it possible to put aside her role in our moral formation and political thought, then it seems we have misunderstood what the church's motherhood means to us.

It's an area of sometimes dim understanding that Pope Francis has seemed especially intent on illuminating. From the earliest days of his papacy, the Holy Father has placed special emphasis on the church's motherhood. The metaphor is one of the oldest in Christian history—a favourite of some of the earliest church writers, including St. Cyprian, St. Gregory of Nazianzus, and St. Augustine. The way we think of motherhood now, in our era of widely dispersed parental duties and variegate family forms, is perhaps distant from how early Christians likely thought of the role, and it supplies us with little in the way of imagination. If the church's motherhood means that her role is mainly sentimental, as the '61 usage implies, then we've vastly misunderstood. Paying close attention to Pope Francis's use of the term helps unearth the rich meaning carried in this ancient allegory.

Pope Francis lauds, rightly, the maternal character of the church and the sense of warmth and security our membership in the Body of Christ grants us. "Our Mother Mary and our Mother Church know how to caress their children and show tenderness," he said in his September 15, 2015 morning homily. "To think of the Church without that motherly feeling is to think of a rigid association, an association without human warmth, an orphan."

But a sense of comforting belonging isn't the only thing a mother supplies. "In our catecheses, we have often noted that we do not become a Christian on our own, but by being born and nurtured in the faith in the midst of the People of God, that is the Church," Pope Francis told pilgrims during a September 2014 general audience. "She is a true mother who gives us life in Christ and, in the communion of the Holy Spirit, brings us into a common life with our brothers and sisters." He went on: "As a mother, the Church nurtures us throughout life by illuminating our path with the light of the Gospel and by sustaining us with the Sacraments, especially the Eucharist."

Francis locates a continuity between the Blessed Virgin and the church itself, with both acting as mothers to the Body of Christ: the virgin in bearing, nursing, and raising Jesus; and the church, likewise, *bearing* Christians through the sacrament of baptism, nourishing them through the Eucharist, and raising them with instruction in the Gospel. It seems impossible, in Francis's formulation, to fully participate in one aspect of the life of the church without participating in the others: each element is mutually reinforcing, and steeped in the mystery of the sacraments. To limit one's understanding of the role of a mother—it's emotional, yes, but also physical, and heavily educational—is, therefore, to misread Marian tradition, as well as the role of the church in the world.

The reverse reading—deriving a properly Franciscan reading of the church through his understanding of the Blessed Virgin—also helps to illuminate the wide-ranging nature of motherhood in the pope's imagination. For Francis, Mary is a deeply pedagogical figure. "She teaches us the virtue of waiting even when everything appears meaningless," he told a general audience in May 2017, adding that Mary's steadfastness also teaches us to hope.

Motherhood, for Francis, also takes on a strongly defensive character: Mothers protect their children at all costs, and here, too, the image of

Mary helps illuminate his view. "The Church has the courage of a mother who knows she must defend her children against the dangers which arise from Satan's presence in the world," Francis said in the September 2014 general audience. There are glimmers, here, of Mary standing triumphant on the serpent's head, which communicates both the church's central role in opposing evil as an institution and through the spiritual betterment of its members, and the eschatological destiny of the church in the kingdom of God.

Pope Francis summons for us an image of the church-as-mother that offers maternal comfort and vital instruction, an organic bond and an aspiration of greater worldly fraternity, an origin of our truest selves and a destination for who we will become as Christians. It is no surprise that, under Francis's papacy, mothers in the church have felt recognized and uplifted by his approach to motherhood, benefiting from the Holy Father's emphasis on the dignity and richness of maternity. Through his teaching and example, Francis directs us towards a church that both leads and loves, is both vast and intimate.

Elizabeth Stoker Bruenig is an assistant editor at The Washington Post, *an essayist on Christianity and politics, and a wife and mother.*

Clerical abuse

Francis Sullivan

The clerical sexual abuse scandal has laid bare crimes and complicity within the Catholic Church. Not only has the extent of the abuse been concealed, so too has its handling by bishops and their superiors.

This deeply ingrained instinct for institutional survival has dominated the hierarchy's mentality and approach to this scandal. Even Pope Francis has struggled to shake loose from this mindset.

Francis seems compassionate towards victims but too often has expressed sympathy for and been lenient with bishops without recourse to the impact on the abuse survivors. Only after public outrage demanding a different attitude has he changed course, sometimes hastily, but at least in the right direction.

Previous pontificates have tried to manage the fallout of the scandal through a minimalist strategy. Rarely were they proactive, nor were they prepared to acknowledge the extent of episcopal irresponsibility and complicity. They sought to conceal the extent of the abuse until under relentless public scrutiny they shifted to a containment approach leaving blame exclusively with errant priests. Admitting to the blatant concealment and cover-ups designed to protect the image of the church, and at times the perpetrators themselves, was a bridge too far.

Early into his pontificate Francis took deliberate steps to set a new course in addressing the scandal. He knew words would not be enough and in 2013 established the Pontifical Commission for the Protection of Minors. Its brief was limited and it has had modest results. Yet it shows his resolve to instigate institutional changes.

By July 2014, Pope Francis was beginning to acknowledge the degree to which bishops had mishandled the crisis. In a Mass at the Vatican's Domus Sanctae Marthae attended by victims of clerical abuse, he said: "I beg your forgiveness, too, for the sins of omission on the part of church leaders who did not respond adequately to reports of abuse . . . this led to even greater suffering on the part of those who were abused and it endangered other minors who were at risk."

Yet, still he only went so far. There was no acknowledgement of those cultural factors within the church that protect it at all costs and in turn the careers of those in positions of power and privilege.

After such a promising start what has confounded observers is the way the pope seems to slip back at times into a more defensive and an "institution-first" approach.

This was reflected in his address to the US bishops in September 2015. Here he sought to side with the travails of the bishops rather than being unequivocally with the plight of victims.

"I realize how much the pain of recent years has weighed upon you," he said and went on to say, "and I have supported your generous commitment to bring healing to victims—in the knowledge that in healing we too are healed—and to work to ensure that such crimes will never be repeated."

Curiously, whereas he has berated the clergy over the evils of clericalism, he hasn't used major public occasions to challenge the episcopacy over the history of denials and cover-ups that has so damaged the very image of the church they sought to protect.

Maybe it is an indication of the weight of resistance within the Curia to his reforms that the pope has been caught in messy public relations blow-ups. Deliberately or otherwise he has been poorly advised. The sense of leniency that has accompanied his approach to the Italian paedophile Fr. Mauro Inzoli or the Chilean bishop Juan Barros is far from convincing that the Vatican fully understands the gravity of the situation. So, too, the contradictory way in which some priests are defrocked whilst others are banished to a monastery for prayer and penance for seemingly similar crimes against children. It seems that little thought has been given to what a pontiff should say and do for people confused by the history of mixed messages coming from the Vatican over moral integrity and the welfare of children. Or it is more of the same institutional self-preservation no matter what.

The story of Pope Francis and the abuse scandal is still unfolding. It is odd that such a good social communicator has not spoken often enough about the biggest scandal for the church in the Western world. Neither has he taken the opportunity to regularly meet with victims on his travels. Sadly, there has not even been a symbolic washing of the feet of victims at a Holy Thursday ceremony.

A balanced assessment of the pope's perspective needs to acknowledge his push to instigate accountability for bishops in safeguarding the welfare of children. Again he has run up against clerical resistance: firstly, within the Congregation for the Doctrine of the Faith and then from some luke-warm responses across the world's episcopal conferences. To his credit he has persisted, and only time will tell if he has a strategy beyond what we have seen so far.

It must be noted that for a response to clerical abuse that can satisfy the scrutiny of integrity and honesty, the church itself must pass muster.

The degree to which Pope Francis appreciates the cultural factors in the church that have led to and sustained the scandal is still a moot point. Taking decisive steps to demonstrate that it is not "business as usual" must become characteristic of his style.

To that end, the signs are hopeful. Be it a sign of his own awakening or an indication of his frustration, the pope has become more explicit and candid about the irresponsibility of the church over the sex abuse scandal. This was made plain in his December 28, 2016, letter to the world's bishops where he states: "It is a sin that shames us. People responsible for the protection of those children destroyed their dignity. We regret this deeply and we beg for forgiveness. We join in the pain of the victims and weep for this sin. The sin of what happened, the sin of failing to help, the sin of covering up and denial, the sin of the abuse of power."

These are the words the world has waited to hear. They are words of a leader who not only feels the pain of victims but is prepared to wear the shame of the hypocrisy of his church. In speaking in this way, the Holy Father shows that this miserable wound can only be healed once all the truth is out and the causes of the scandal are fully revealed and dealt with.

Francis Sullivan is the chief executive of Australia's Truth, Justice and Healing Council. Previously he was secretary general of the Australian Medical Association and chief executive of Catholic Health Australia. He has degrees in theology and politics and is an adjunct professor at the Australian Catholic University, Canberra.

Clericalism

Archbishop Paul-André Durocher

Every year the president, vice-president, and secretary general of the Canadian Conference of Catholic Bishops spend a few days in Rome visiting various curial officials and meeting with the pope. One year when I was president, our secretary general—a priest—was sick and had to be replaced by our assistant secretary general, a layman. A few moments before our papal audience, we were told the assistant secretary general could greet Pope Francis and have his picture taken with him, but would not be allowed to attend the meeting since he was not ordained. The vice president and I insisted, explaining that he had been ASG for over twenty years and had kept more pontifical secrets than anyone else in Canada. We were told the pope would be asked, and we were delighted when he agreed.

As the four of us took our chairs, Pope Francis said something like this to us: "They asked me if your ASG could sit in on our meeting. I asked why not? They said he wasn't ordained. I asked, 'Is he baptized? Of course he can join our meeting.' I am glad you have named a layman to such a position of responsibility in your episcopal conference. Clericalism is a disease which weakens our church." Then he turned to our ASG and said directly to him, "I am glad you are a layman." To which our ASG replied, "And I am glad you are the pope!" We all burst out laughing.

For Pope Francis, clericalism goes to the heart of the sometimes problematic relationship between the clergy and the laity within the Catholic Church. He is not the first pope to address this issue, of course.

Back in 1946, in a speech to the cardinals he had newly created, Pope Pius XII commented, "Within the church, there exist not an active and passive element, leadership and lay people. All members of the church are called to work on the perfection of the body of Christ. . . . [Lay believers] ought to have an ever-clearer consciousness not only of belonging to the church, but of being the church, that is to say, the community of the faithful on earth under the leadership of the pope, the common head, and of the bishops in communion with him. They are the church."

The Second Vatican Council would ground this teaching in the common dignity of all the baptized and would roll out its implications in many of its documents, particularly *Lumen Gentium* (on the church) and *Apostolicam Actuositatem* (on the lay apostolate). Pope John Paul II devoted a synod and an exhortation (*Christifideles Laici*) to this issue. However, nearly seventy-five years after Pope Pius XII's encyclical letter on the church, *Mystici Corporis*, Pope Francis considers that church teaching on the full participation of the lay faithful in the church's life has yet to be realized. As he said in a letter to Cardinal Marc Ouellet dated March 19, 2016: "I remember now the famous expression: 'It's the time of the laity,' but it seems that the clock has stopped."

His pastoral experience as archbishop of Buenos Aires led him to identify certain attitudes that impede the full flowering of the charisms of many lay faithful within the church. A few months after his election to the Petrine ministry, he diagnosed the problem this way in a speech to the bishops of Latin America: "Clericalism . . . has to do with a sinful complicity: the priest clericalizes the layperson and the layperson kindly asks to be clericalized, because deep down it is easier. . . . This in part explains the lack of maturity and of Christian freedom of a part of the laity." He pointed out that the problem does not only lie with clergy who are tempted to hold on to their power, but also with the laity who do not want to be burdened with the responsibility of full engagement with the church's life.

Indeed, resisting the temptation of clericalism is demanding for both clergymen and laypeople. It requires true collaboration, a sharing in power and the development of new decision-making processes. Pope Francis gave three examples of this new direction in his talk to the Latin American bishops: "The spread of bible study groups, of ecclesial [base] communities and of Pastoral Councils is in fact helping to overcome clericalism and to increase lay responsibility."

According to Francis, clericalism not only impedes the Christian growth of laypeople, it distorts the clergy itself, distancing deacons, priests, and bishops from the people, leading to the institutionalization of the church, causing great harm. In his sermon on the morning of December 13, 2016, in the chapel at Domus Sanctae Marthae, he lamented the attitude of the priestly caste in Jesus' time. They had no regard for those entrusted to them, "a humble people, cast aside and browbeaten by these individuals." Still today, he said, "clergymen feel superior; they distance themselves from the people; they have no time to listen to the poor, the suffering, the prisoners, the sick. . . . Clericalism is truly an awful reality, and its victim is always the same: the poor, humble people that wait for the Lord."

There is another side to clericalism that bothers Pope Francis: the tendency to make clerics of lay leaders. In March 2014, speaking to the members of *Corallo*, an Italian network of Catholic radio and television stations, he recalled his experience in Buenos Aires: "I've heard this so often in my homeland, 'In my parish, there's a really fine layman who knows how to organize. . . . Eminence, why don't we make him a deacon?' Right away, this is the priest's suggestion: clericalize. . . . And why? Is the deacon or the priest more important? No! This is an error. . . . He's a good layman? Then let him continue as such and grow as such. Because this involves the identity of Christian belonging. For me, clericalism impedes the growth of the laity."

Here, the pope berates a lack of appreciation for the specific vocation of the laity, a belittling of the laity's mission within the church and the world. He frowns on an attitude that implies that only ordained ministry has value and importance. A committed, empowered laity is key to developing a missionary church, one that is truly able to proclaim the "Joy of the Gospel" to today's world.

This helps us understand his doubts about choosing women as cardinals or ordaining women to the diaconate. Speaking of the first, he was quoted in the Italian daily *La Stampa* as saying, "I don't know where this funny idea comes from. Women in the church must be valued, not 'clericalized.' Whoever thinks of women cardinals suffers from a bit of clericalism." And at his meeting with the International Union of Superiors General in May 2016, although he agreed to set up a commission to study the history of women deacons in the church, he again spoke about the danger of clericalizing both lay men and women.

Obviously, this begs the question of why it would be right to ordain some men to the permanent diaconate if that is their vocation, while ordaining women would automatically mean giving in to clericalization. On the other hand, the pope often speaks of the need to open up the church's power structure to women, without necessarily giving them clerical functions. This, in turn, raises the issue of the bond between the power of orders and the power of governance in the church. That, however, would require a whole other article.

Archbishop Paul-André Durocher leads the Archdiocese of Gatineau, Quebec.

Collegiality

Archbishop Mark Coleridge

I did a fair bit of media commentary on the conclave that elected Pope Francis. This was no mean feat, given that the election happened in the middle of the Australian night and I was roused from sleep to utter media-friendly profundities about a new pope of whom I knew little. Like many others, I was deeply impressed by the new pope's first words and gestures on the balcony of St. Peter's. But that was all on television long before dawn.

The first time I saw and met Pope Francis in person was at the end of a Vatican meeting. We were herded into the *Sala Clementina* in the usual style and took our seats for what we thought would be a long wait. The audience was scheduled for noon, but normally the audiences got later as the morning wore on. So we expected the noon audience to begin about 12:30. I was chatting to the bishop next to me when all of a sudden the pope entered—at 11:50. We were all caught on the hop. Normally the pope entered the hall in stately style, waved discreetly at those gathered who responded with respectful applause as the pontiff moved to his seat on a dais up at the front. But not this time.

Pope Francis entered the hall casually and began shaking hands with the cardinals up at the front. The rest of us weren't sure how to respond to this—all the more so given that we'd already noticed that his seat wasn't on a dais. It was on the same level as us. Eventually the pope began to give his speech, but he departed regularly from his text—and the asides were more interesting than the text. He was actually talking to us, even talking *with* us. At the end he left the hall, but again not as we expected. Instead of sweeping out to the applause of those gathered, he once more shook a few hands and exchanged a few words. He then left the hall but almost immediately reappeared. He wanted to speak to someone else. We weren't sure whether to applaud or not. This happened twice, and it left us all with heads spinning after an audience that had overturned all the protocols as we'd known them—and having worked for a time in the papal court, I knew them well. The whole thing was uncourtly, fraternal, relaxed, and *collegial* in a way we hadn't seen coming.

Some time later I was again in Rome at the 2015 synod. I'd been at a synod before and knew the ropes. I knew that the members gathered in the Synod Hall and that the pope entered once we were all assembled. He entered to applause and took his seat in the middle up at the front. That was the protocol, and it's what I expected this time. But one day early on as I arrived I saw Pope Francis walking from Casa Santa Marta with one of the cardinals, bag in one hand and umbrella in the other. No big black car with flags flying; no swarm of minders. Just a man in a white coat doing what the rest of us did as we gathered for the day's work. He entered the foyer of the Paul VI Hall and spoke to a few bishops—just like the rest of us. He then took the elevator to the hall above, stood up at the front near his seat and greeted all kinds of people as they entered the hall. With some, it was a cheery greeting, with others he was clearly doing business. But again it said, "I'm one of you. I'm a bishop among bishops." And we weren't used to that. It was collegiality in a new and disarmingly simple key.

This happened day after day, and I was deeply impressed by it. It struck me after a while that it in no way diminished the Petrine ministry. Paradoxically, it showed the papacy in greater relief. It certainly didn't stop the voice of Peter sounding at key moments through the synod. I think of his speeches at the celebration of the fifty years of the Synod of Bishops and at the synod's end. It was Jorge Mario Bergoglio who spoke, but we heard the voice of Peter—as surely as they did in Acts 15. A more collegial style enhanced rather than diminished the authority of the office. A pope who was one of us could speak to the assembly with an authority belonging to him alone but providing a service to us all. In speaking of the need for what he called "a healthy decentralization," Francis could speak the language of collegiality without undermining or abandoning the primacy of Peter.

This, it might be thought, is more a matter of style than substance. But consider John O'Malley's remarks on Vatican II:

> The style of Vatican II is different: this is the clue indicating the significance of the council. It defined nothing. It legislated little. To accomplish the goals of the council, the documents appeal to the good will of those to whom they are directed and therefore strive to motivate them to heartfelt acceptance. The documents read more like invitations than injunctions. The new style is profoundly significant and . . . goes to the heart of the council. The council is about style. We tend to think of style as ornamentation, "mere rhetoric." Yet on a deeper level we know well that content and mode of expression are inextricably intertwined, that there is no thought without expression, and expression is what style is all about ("A Break from the Past," *Commonweal*, March 9, 2001).

To think that either Vatican II or Pope Francis is only about style as ornamentation is to get both wrong. I've given a couple of instances of Pope Francis's more collegial style, but make no mistake about it—these are about substance. This is collegiality not as an arcane theological term. It's collegiality beyond concepts and words, collegiality in action—the kind of action that everyone can understand.

It's becoming clearer as this pontificate unfolds that the monarchical papacy is at an end. The monarchical form of the papacy emerged under particular historical circumstances and served its purpose for a long time. But its time has now passed. Pope Francis is moving to dismantle the papal court, the historical roots of which reach deep and wide and the cultural embeddedness of which is formidable. It's clear to me that this goes to the heart of Vatican II. It's also clear, I think, that this epochal shift is under the impulse of the Holy Spirit, blowing from the depths of the perfect collegiality that we usually call the Trinity.

Archbishop Mark Coleridge leads the Archdiocese of Brisbane, Australia. He was a member of the 2015 Synod on the Vocation and Mission of the Family in the Church and in the Contemporary World.

Conscience

Austen Ivereigh

The words in paragraph 37 of *Amoris Laetitia*, Pope Francis's great exhortation on love in marriage and family, are few, yet clear as a fresh dawn, heralding a revolution. "We have been called to form consciences," Francis says, "not replace them."

The Jesuit moral theologian Fr. James Keenan called these words "sensational" in an April 21, 2017, article for *Crux*. Cardinal Christoph Schönborn of Vienna, whom Francis asked to present *Amoris Laetitia* to the media when it came out in 2016, says he was "deeply moved" when he read them. "Do we *really* trust in the consciences of people who often respond as best they can?" he asked, searchingly, during a July 2017 lecture in Limerick, Ireland, before adding: "The *bonum possibile* in moral theology is an important concept that has been so often neglected."

All true reform in the church, as Yves Congar noted in his classic treatment of the topic back in 1950, involves not the taking on of something alien from the outside, but the re-integration of something of the church's own that went astray. In restoring the proper place of conscience to discern God's call, Francis is not importing from contemporary subjectivism or situation ethics but from St. Thomas Aquinas and the Second Vatican Council.

It's hard to pinpoint exactly when or where conscience went AWOL, except that it had happened by the time of St. John Paul II's great 1993 hymn to the objectivity of truth, *Veritatis Splendor*. There was a fear at the time among moral theologians, recalled Schönborn in Limerick, that the link between the church's teaching and conscience would be weakened by the onslaught of situation ethics, so the stress was on the immutability of law and doctrine.

These are, of course, vital. Conscience, as Francis reminds us in paragraph 300 of *Amoris Laetitia*, needs humility, docility, a love for the church and her eternal teaching and "can never prescind from the Gospel demands of truth and charity." Yet in that process of warding off the threat of relativism, "conscience became caricatured as being right when it is the transposition of the church's teaching into acts," said Schönborn. There was a tendency to reduce God's will to the parameters of church teaching and law, and the role of conscience to working out simply how to follow these.

"We have long thought that simply by stressing doctrinal, bioethical and moral issues, without encouraging openness to grace, we were providing sufficient support to families," Francis begins paragraph 37 in *Amoris*. But it hasn't been enough. Families have collapsed. As Keenan notes, the question has not been so much whether conscience leaves people free to ignore church teaching, but how much church teaching informs the regular decisions of the Catholic conscience. Francis wants to throw a rope over that ravine.

Conscience is "the most secret core and sanctuary" of a person, where he "is alone with God, whose voice echoes in his depths," as *Gaudium et Spes* paragraph 16 puts it. There we encounter truth, and the truth about God is both his mercy and his judgment. Conscience is not a way of evading the law, but of discovering God's will. "The work of conscience is to discover that God's law resonates in my life," as Schönborn put it in Limerick. "It is not a foreign law imposed on me but it is the discovery that God's will for me and God's law for humanity is what is best for me."

But this must be, Schönborn stresses, "an interior discovery." The word associated with conscience in the Hebrew Bible is *kardia*, "heart," meaning not the bodily organ but the seat of our affectivity and desires. The "law of the Spirit" of which Aquinas speaks is what flows from knowing God's love. Thus, for example, fidelity in marriage is not an external rule imposed on me but what love demands; it is written by God within the human heart. The church's task is to help people experience that love so that they can better form their conscience, which means to make room in their lives for God's grace and to decide on the action that follows.

Without grace—God's invitation, and his assistance—the high ideals of marriage or anything else can be forbidding, even discouraging.

As synod father Msgr. Phillipe Bordeyne, rector of the Catholic Institute in Paris, puts it, the programme of *Amoris* is "to help people better respond to the offer of grace." To form consciences, as Francis asks of the church, he says, "you must awaken people to the sweet presence in them of grace, which bathes their limitations in a light of mercy in such a way that the decisions they are to take become at the same time more audacious and more realistic" (*Divorcés Remariés: Ce qui change avec François* [Paris: Salvator, 2017], 24–25).

As the furious reaction to *Amoris* has made obvious, for some this smacks of a capitulation. This is true notably in the United States, where the most rabid and disrespectful Catholic opposition to Pope Francis has its bunker. Is it partly cultural? The American use of conscience "never really settled into, nor emerged from the place it did in Europe, that is, as the source of responsible personal and social moral agency," Keenan pointed out in a January 2, 2017, article in *America* magazine. It was what you invoked to opt out of a law or rule, which is what the cardinal authors who are challenging *Amoris* fear when they ask in point five of their September 2016 letter to Francis containing *dubia* if the exhortation excludes "a creative interpretation of the role of conscience."

Their reasoning illustrates how, in combatting a threat, you can be defined and corrupted by it, so you no longer see things as they obviously are. Conscience in *Amoris* is not an opt-out of the law and teaching but an opt-in to their application to concrete situations. It requires what Jesuits call discernment and the classical Thomist tradition calls the virtue of prudence. It calls for accompaniment—pastoral closeness—on the part of the priest, who helps the believer to see that despite the limits in which he or she is operating, God is at work in their lives, and that by the power of his grace they can always take concrete steps. Conscience allows people to form a right judgment in the reality where they are rather than in the ideal where they ought to be, and plots a course between them.

That's what it means in *Amoris* 37 when Francis speaks of the faithful responding to the Gospel "amidst their limitations." A person's limitations—the boundaries of their existence, that often they are powerless to control—are unique, and only knowable to those close to the situation. As Pope Francis's amanuensis, Archbishop Víctor Manuel Fernández of the Pontifical Catholic University of Argentina, puts it in a 2011 article whose theology of grace has clearly influenced *Evangelii Gaudium* 171 and *Amoris Laetitia* 301, a person can falter in the exercise of the virtues because of forms of conditioning or circumstance that diminish their culpability ("Vida trinitaria, normas éticas y fragilidad humana. Algunas breves precisiones," *Universitas* No. 6 [2011], Universidad Católica Argentina).

That's why, as Francis puts it in *Amoris*, "simply to consider whether or not an individual's actions correspond to a general law or rule"—that is, the approach of the *dubia* cardinals—"is not enough to discern and ensure full fidelity to God in the concrete life of a human being" (AL 304).

Hence the programme: "individual conscience needs to be better incorporated into the church's praxis," as the pope notes in *Amoris* 303. This is not to expect less of people. Francis is a demanding pope. Neither idealism nor despair—both cop-outs—is now on the cards. Francis is the teacher of the divine pedagogy of the little steps, the ones that forge the path forward that God's grace, through the exercise of conscience, lights up.

In the *villas miseria* of Buenos Aires, Francis saw grace at work in lives that were far from the church's ideal, lives burdened by the limits and constraints of dehumanizing poverty and violence. He met Christ in their wounds. He saw how poor folk, imbued by grace, strove for the good, and how a little step towards God under such circumstances can be more valuable than moral probity under comfortable circumstances.

Conscience, properly formed by the church, recognizes and bridges such gaps: between our loving Creator and us, between this world and the next, between who we are and what we are called to be.

That's why its recovery is among the greatest achievements of the Francis papacy.

Austen Ivereigh is a British journalist and commentator, contributing editor of Crux, *and author of a biography of Pope Francis,* The Great Reformer: Francis and the Making of a Radical Pope *(Picador, 2015). He is also founder and director of the church media project Catholic Voices.*

Creation

John Chryssavgis

"Creation is of the order of love. God's love is the
fundamental moving force in all created things."
—*Laudato Si'* 77

"United by the Same Concern"

It was a unique privilege for me to attend the formal publication of
the green encyclical issued by Pope Francis. *Laudato Si': On Care for our
Common Home* was released before a crowded audience in the new synod
hall of the Vatican on June 18, 2015.

The occasion was both historical and ecumenical. It marked the first
time that a papal encyclical cited—indeed, highlighted—an Orthodox
prelate, Ecumenical Patriarch Bartholomew (LS 7–9). It was also the first
time that a papal document was jointly launched at the Vatican by a senior
cardinal of a Roman Catholic authority, Peter Turkson, together with a
senior and distinguished hierarch theologian of the Orthodox Church,
Metropolitan John [Zizioulas] of Pergamon. This was an extraordinarily
unprecedented moment and a profound ecumenical gesture on the part
of Pope Francis.

When in March of 2013 Ecumenical Patriarch Bartholomew attended
the inaugural mass of Pope Francis, his spontaneous initiative signalled
the first time that the leader of either church had ever participated in such
an event. One year prior to the launching of *Laudato Si'*, the pope and

the patriarch also shared a pilgrimage to the Holy Land, where they celebrated the fiftieth anniversary of the visit there in 1964 by their visionary predecessors, Paul VI and Athenagoras. In many ways, then, the papal encyclical on creation care was long anticipated from the perspective of ecumenical openness between the two sister churches and their respective leaders, who were "united by the same concern."

The broad perspective of creation as "our common home" is a reminder that the ecological crisis is larger than any single individual or institution, larger than any single denomination or faith, and larger than the world itself. The proper remedy for our excess consumption is the awareness that earth belongs to heaven (LS 67), the acknowledgment that neither material possessions, nor the air and the sea, can be claimed by the few.

A Crisis of the Spirit

Both Pope Francis and Patriarch Bartholomew have repeatedly emphasized that the predicament we face is not primarily ecological but essentially spiritual (LS 101). "Human life is grounded in three fundamental and closely intertwined relationships: with God, with our neighbour and with the earth itself. According to the Bible, these three vital relationships have been broken. . . . This rupture is sin" (LS 66). It is a crisis concerning the way we regard and relate to the world. We treat the natural environment in an inhumane, godless manner because we perceive it in this way. "In calling to mind the figure of Saint Francis of Assisi, we come to realize that a healthy relationship with creation is one dimension of overall personal conversion, which entails the recognition of our errors, sins, faults and failures, and leads to heartfelt repentance and desire to change" (LS 218).

Another ancient response to sin is asceticism, whose intrinsic value is properly understood in the spirit of freedom and gratitude; its ultimate purpose is the rediscovery of wonder in the created world. The goal of asceticism is moderation, not repression; it looks to service and not selfishness. Asceticism is about living simply and about simply living. Without asceticism, none of us is authentically human.

The Cry of the Earth

The response, then, to today's "throwaway culture" (LS 20–22) is to recognize in the face of the world the face of my brother and sister, and in the face of the earth the very face of God. This is why *Laudato Si'* quotes St. Bonaventure describing his mystic mentor, St. Francis of Assisi: "Filled with abundant piety, he would call creatures, no matter how small, by the name of 'brother' or 'sister'" (LS 10–12). We will resolve the ecological crisis only when we recognize in all animals (LS 32–42), each tree (LS 39) and every body of water (LS 27–31) a face, a place, and a voice that longs to be heard.

Of course, this takes a generous act of sacrifice and grace. The cry of the earth is ultimately a call for humility. Pride is a uniquely human attribute; it belongs to Adam (LS 67)! "The harmony between the Creator, humanity and creation as a whole was disrupted by our presuming to take the place of God and refusing to acknowledge our creaturely limitations" (LS 66). All other species seem instinctively to know where they fit in the order of things (LS 68). It is a matter of doing with less. Surely this is what the "sabbath" principle (LS 71) is all about.

The Cry of the Poor

When we travel light, we are attuned to the cry of the poor. For we respond to nature with the same tenderness with which we respond to people (LS 66). The ecumenical movement aptly coined the term *eco-justice*: all ecological activities and economic programmes, all theological principles and spiritual practices are ultimately measured by their effect on people, especially the poor (cf. Matt 25:31). As the papal encyclical puts it: "A true ecological approach . . . must integrate questions of justice . . . so as to hear both the cry of the earth and the cry of the poor" (LS 49).

We must hear the voice of the poor. We must affirm the dignity of the poor. We must assume responsibility for the consequences of our actions on the poor. Our market is based on exploitation and exclusion; our technology marginalizes and excludes the poor. The first word in any ecological response comes less from the environment or even from theology; it comes from our attitude to the poor (LS 48–52).

This is perhaps why, on the day of his election, the pope assumed the name Francis, an unmistakable indication of his priority for and sensitivity to the vulnerable and the oppressed in our global community. In his encyclical, he prays: "O God, bring healing to our lives, that we may protect the world and not prey on it. . . . Touch the hearts of those who look only for gain at the expense of the poor" (LS 246).

What Pope Francis and Patriarch Bartholomew reminded and reinforced is that preserving nature and serving neighbour are inseparably interrelated. Both leaders have repeatedly underlined the intimate connection between environmental and social justice, declaring solidarity with people suffering from war and persecution, as well as poverty and hunger.

"Integral Ecology" and "Ecological Conversion"

This approach is a breath of fresh air in a world that has long regarded the church as a strict and static institution. Theologians may understand *what the church is*; but Francis and Bartholomew underline *where the church should be*! By re-centring the priority of the church, Francis and Bartholomew provide a personal face to its vocation.

The favourable reception of—and, paradoxically, the adverse reaction to—the way in which Pope Francis (with his "green encyclical") and Patriarch Bartholomew (with his "green ministry") advocate for creation care is arguably the greatest proof that they are on the right track.

The world is not hungry simply for bread (Matt 6:10); it is hungry for a sense of holiness and mystery, for a spiritual vision that does not lose sight of the trees, the poor, or the sacred. This in turn endows us with a sense of integrity for life and the natural environment. It inspires an understanding of the reconciliation of all people and all things. And it restores the covenant between God and creation, so that God's will may be "done, on earth as in heaven" (Matt 6:10).

Rev. Dr. John Chryssavgis is Archdeacon of the Ecumenical Patriarchate and theological adviser to Ecumenical Patriarch Bartholomew on environmental issues. He lives in Harpswell, Maine, and serves as theologian to the Ecumenical Office of the Greek Orthodox Archdiocese of America.

Curia

Massimo Faggioli

A reflection on Pope Francis's use of the word "curia" is an interesting exploration in the relationship between a very popular pope and a very unpopular institution of the Roman Catholic Church, although its unpopularity is not always for legitimate reasons. It is also an interesting exploration between an outsider like Francis and the ultimate symbol of "insiderness."

Francis has used the phrase "Roman Curia" many times but considerably less than his immediate predecessors, for one simple reason: his predecessors had to interact more frequently with it. John XXIII had to use the Vatican bureaucracy for the preparation of the Second Vatican Council between 1959 and 1962. Paul VI and John Paul II pursued reforms of the institution in 1967 and 1988, respectively. Benedict XVI, living in Rome as cardinal prefect of the Congregation for the Doctrine of the Faith from 1982 until his election in 2005, had worked in and known the Curia for a long time.

Francis's distance from the Curia is not just a matter of words, but also of style of governing the church. The "outsiderness" of Francis from the Roman, clerical hierarchy is visible in the rarity of his exercise of the institutional chain of command between the pope and the congregations of the Curia, led by cardinals and archbishops. Francis governs mostly without them.

Francis talks to the Curia also—if not especially—through the media, and there is a very interesting way the pope does so. The most important examples of Francis's way of using the word "Curia" are in his three addresses to the leaders of the Vatican bureaucracy, given to them in remarks around Christmas time in 2014, 2015, and 2016.

In the speech of December 21, 2015, Francis explained his vision of the Curia with an acrostic analysis of the Italian word for mercy: *misericordia*. The pope said that sixteenth-century Italian Jesuit Fr. Matteo Ricci had done something similar during his missionary work in China and that he wanted to share the analysis "with the aim of having it serve as our guide and beacon."

The twelve-letter acrostic does not translate exactly into English, but the Vatican listed the English equivalents as: **M**issionary and pastoral spirit; **I**doneity and sagacity; **S**pirituality and humanity; **E**xample and fidelity; **R**easonableness and gentleness; **I**nnocuousness and determination; **C**harity and truth; **O**penness and maturity; **R**espectfulness and humility; **D**iligence and attentiveness; **I**ntrepidness and alertness; **A**ccountability and sobriety.

The 2016 speech was more directly aimed at encouraging the Curia to "reform" in the sense of changing, redirecting, confirming, and transforming. "Here I spontaneously think of the ancient adage that describes the process of the Spiritual Exercises in the Ignatian method," said Francis, listing in Latin the four actions described by Jesuit founder St. Ignatius of Loyola: "*deformata reformare, reformata conformare, conformata confirmare et confirmata transformare*."

Most interestingly, Francis was not shy in 2016 in saying in public that there was a need for the Curia not only to "*con-form* to the Good News" and to "*con-form* to the signs of our times and to all its human achievements," but also of "*con-forming* . . . ever more fully to its purpose, which is that of cooperating in the ministry of the Successor of Peter" and "supporting the Roman Pontiff in the exercise of his singular, ordinary, full, supreme, immediate and universal power."

This encouragement was substantiated by a list of guiding principles, which is usual for Francis's speeches to the Curia. The principles given in 2016 were: individual responsibility, pastoral concern, missionary spirit, organizational clarity, improved functioning, modernization, sobriety, subsidiarity, synodality, catholicity, professionalism, and gradualism.

In some ways, however, the most interesting words given by Francis to the Curia came in December 2014 because of the way he described the Curia itself.

In that speech, the pope famously warned the bureaucracy of fifteen diseases he had seen in their work and attitudes: thinking they are "immortal," "immune," or downright "indispensable"; the "Martha complex," or excessive busy-ness; mental and spiritual "petrification"; excessive planning and of functionalism; poor coordination; "spiritual Alzheimer's"; rivalry and vainglory; existential schizophrenia; gossiping, grumbling, and back-biting; idolizing superiors; indifference to others; lugubriousness; hoarding; closed circles; seeking worldly profit, and forms of self-exhibition.

But the 2014 speech is especially remarkable for a section at the beginning of the address in which Francis described his ecclesiology of the Roman Curia. He said: "It is attractive to think of the Roman Curia as a small-scale model of the church, in other words, as a 'body' which strives seriously every day to be more alive, more healthy, more harmonious and more united in itself and with Christ." This passage is noteworthy because one of the key problems of the Curia has been that it has a very weak tie to theological legitimacy, besides the claim of its historic institutional and political functions.

Here the pope tries to describe the Roman Curia as a "small-scale model of the church," clearly setting aside the fact that it is fundamentally lacking a basis in ecclesiology and disregarding the differences between, for example, the very diverse sociology of the global church today and the almost totally clerical sociology of the Curia.

What is particularly interesting are the ways in which Francis differs from his predecessors in how he talks to and about the Roman Curia. In the history of modern Catholicism and especially during the last century, one main worry of the Roman pontiffs has always been to reassure members of the Curia as growing calls for its reform were made. Between Pius X (in 1908) and John Paul II (in 1988), all popes—except Francis and, for obvious reasons, John Paul I—have implemented some kind of reform of the Roman Curia while at the same time reassuring its members in key moments in the life of their pontificates. One example is Paul VI's September 21, 1963, speech at the beginning of his pontificate and of the second session of the Second Vatican Council, in which he called the Curia members "optimal colleagues, collaborators, and unforgettable friends."

Francis's pontificate is different from his predecessors—and has some similarities, at least for once, with Benedict XVI's. Francis's 2014, 2015, and 2016 speeches did not have the goal of reassuring the Curia. But the straightforwardness of Francis's language about the ills of its members is juxtaposed with the lack of an overarching theological or institutional overhaul of the Vatican bureaucracy. Francis communicates his diagnosis of the problems of the Roman Curia through language defining a spiritual experience more than continuing functional mismanagement. This is clearly consistent with Francis's criticism of the "technocratic paradigm" in his 2015 encyclical *Laudato Si'*. It might also disappoint those expecting a comprehensive overhaul of the central government of the Catholic Church during his pontificate.

Massimo Faggioli is a professor of historical theology at Villanova University and contributing editor to Commonweal. *He is the author of many books, published in several languages, on Vatican II, the new Catholic movements, and the papacy. His latest book for Liturgical Press is* Catholicism and Citizenship. Political Cultures of the Church in the Twenty-First Century *(2017).*

Dialogue

Archbishop Roberto O. González Nieves, OFM

> The church . . . lives by dialoguing with
> men and women of every era.
> —general audience, October 22, 2016

Dialogue is one of the most frequent words in the homilies and writings of Pope Francis. For Francis, even evangelization implies a path of dialogue.

According to the pope, three areas of dialogue stand out for the church today—where it must be present in order to promote full human development and to pursue the common good: with states; with society, including with cultures and the sciences; and with other believers who are not part of the Catholic Church (*Evangelii Gaudium* 238).

For Francis, dialogue has a fundamental place in evangelization, coupled with docility to the call of the Lord and the power of grace (homily, May 8, 2014). The centrality of dialogue in the life of the church is masterfully set out in *Evangelii Gaudium*, where Francis exposes in various sections the fundamentals of evangelization in our times.

For example, the pope encourages the church to privilege social dialogue as a contribution to peace (EG 238–58); to encourage dialogue between faith, reason and the sciences (242–43); to engage in ecumenical dialogue (244–46); to dialogue in its relations with Judaism (247–49); to be a church that pursues interreligious dialogue (250–54); and to be immersed in a social dialogue in a context of religious freedom (255–58).

The pope says dialogue is not something we can take for granted. Dialogue is something that is constructed with three elements: "humility," "meekness," and "becoming all to all." Dialogue needs to take place as soon as possible, and in a dialogue there is no need to raise voices (homily, January 24, 2014). To dialogue is not just to talk; it is knowing how to listen. Dialogue can be dangerous when you close yourself up, get angry, or start fighting.

Francis acknowledges, too, that there are dangers in dialogue. In an August 21, 2013, address to students and teachers from the Seibu Gakuen Junior High School in Japan, the pope warned: "If during a dialogue someone closes up within him- or herself and grows angry, he or she may start a fight; there is the danger of conflict and this is not good, because we talk to each other to find ourselves and not in order to quarrel."

Certain attitudes are required for a true dialogue. These are meekness, the ability to encounter people, to encounter cultures with the hope of establishing peace and the ability to ask intelligent questions. As Francis told the Japanese schoolchildren and teachers: "If you do not think like me—but you know that I think differently, and you do not convince me—we are equally friends, I have heard how you think and you have heard how I think."

Dialogue cannot take place in a vacuum; it has to take place in a context, based upon a starting point. What is that starting point? It has to be our own identity as Christians. Without being clear about our identity as Christians we cannot engage in authentic dialogue. During his 2014 visit to South Korea, Francis met with bishops from across Asia. He told them:

> We cannot engage in real dialogue unless we are conscious of our own identity. We cannot dialogue; we cannot start dialoguing from nothing, from zero, from a foggy sense of who we are. Nor can there be authentic dialogue unless we are capable of opening our minds and hearts, in empathy and sincere receptivity, to those with whom we speak. In other words, an attentiveness in which the Holy Spirit is our guide. A clear sense of one's own identity and a capacity for empathy are thus the point of departure for all dialogue. If we are to speak freely, openly and fruitfully with others, we must be clear about who we are, what God has done for us, and what it is that God asks of us. And if our communication is not to be a monologue, there

has to be openness of heart and mind to accepting individuals and cultures. Fearlessly, for fear is the enemy of this kind of openness.

Dialogue also entails certain requirements. One of these is empathy. It is a matter of listening not only to the words spoken by the other, but also to the non-verbal communication of their experiences, their hopes, their aspirations, their difficulties and what really matters to them. This empathy must be the result of our spiritual discernment and personal experience, which makes us see others as brothers and sisters, and listen to their words and works, and beyond these, to what their hearts want to say.

A second requirement is that dialogue must be an act of opening and welcoming the other. I cannot dialogue if the other is closed. Dialogue needs openings.

A third requirement is that dialogue requires acceptance: "Welcome! Come to my home; I welcome you to my heart. My heart welcomes you. My heart wants to listen to you."

Francis visualizes dialogue as a very important aspect of mercy since it allows people to know each other and to understand the demands of one another. Above all, dialogue is a sign of deep respect, because it places people in an attitude of listening and in the condition to welcome the best aspects of one's interlocutor.

Dialogue is also an expression of charity, because, while not ignoring differences, it can help to seek and to share the common good. In addition, dialogue invites us to stand before the other as a gift of God; and this challenges us to identify with the other. Dialogue should give birth to mercy. We do not encounter our neighbour when we want to impose our own views, when we do not listen enough to the other, when we interrupt, when we do not even let the other finish his or her thought. This is not dialogue; rather, this becomes a form of aggression. True dialogue, on the other hand, requires moments of silence in which to welcome the extraordinary gift of the presence of God in the other who is our brother or sister.

As Francis said in his October 22, 2016, general audience, dialogue—when it is authentic, when it is true—is an expression of the great exigency of the love of God, "who goes out to meet everyone and in each one puts a seed of his goodness, so that he can collaborate in his creative work." The pope continued: "Dialogue breaks down the walls of divisions and misunderstandings; it creates bridges of communication and does not allow anyone to isolate or to lock him- or herself in their small world. . . . Listen, explain, docilely, do not yell at the other, nor shout at the other, but have an open heart."

D

Archbishop Roberto O. González Nieves, OFM, leads the Archdiocese of San Juan de Puerto Rico.

Dignity

Tina Beattie

Human dignity is a fundamental principle of Catholic social teaching. The 1948 Universal Declaration of Human Rights begins with an affirmation of inherent human dignity, making this a significant though contested aspect of secular, as well as theological, ethics.

While church teaching consistently defends human dignity in terms of social justice as well as personal morality, in the last few decades it has increasingly focused on sexual and reproductive ethics. Pope Francis shares his predecessors' concerns over such issues, but early in his papacy in an interview with Jesuit Fr. Antonio Spadaro he said the church had become "obsessed" with a focus on single issues such as abortion, gay marriage, and contraception. He is widening the focus to promote an ecologically inclusive concept of dignity, which I would argue constitutes an important and timely doctrinal development.

In approaching this topic, we need to bear in mind the distinction between intrinsic and extrinsic dignity. Intrinsic dignity pertains to the nature of our being. The human person is endowed with the unique dignity that comes with being made in the image of God with a capacity for rationality and freedom that is accorded to no other species. God confers upon all humans "an infinite dignity" (*Evangelii Gaudium* 178) and "no one can strip us of the dignity bestowed upon us by [Christ's] boundless and unfailing love" (EG 3). In expressing the modern church's opposition to the death penalty, Francis says that "not even a murderer loses his personal dignity, and God himself pledges to guarantee this"

(Letter to the President of the International Commission Against the Death Penalty, March 20, 2015).

Extrinsic dignity refers to how we live. It can be enhanced or diminished by our values and lifestyles, and it can be abused or destroyed by external forces. Francis refers to many ways in which dignity is undermined or violated by the selfishness, consumerism, and freneticism of modern life, by the exploitation, abuse, and marginalization of those who are poor, and by neglect and violence towards those who are vulnerable—particularly the unborn and the elderly. To trample on the dignity of another is to trample on one's own dignity. The restoration of dignity is a key theme of his vision for evangelization and the promotion of justice.

To understand how Francis relates human dignity to the rest of creation, we might consider the dignity of work. This has been a significant feature of Catholic social teaching since Pope Leo XIII's 1891 encyclical *Rerum Novarum*, but for Francis it is intimately bound up with the dignity of creation and care for the environment. In his general audience on the feast of St. Joseph the Worker on May 1, 2013 (International Workers' Day), he described human work as sharing in God's work of creation through our vocation "to cultivate and care for all the goods of creation." Metaphorically, work "'anoints' us with dignity, fills us with dignity, makes us similar to God, who has worked and still works," said Francis. To work in a creative, economically just, and environmentally responsible way is an expression of human dignity and a participation in God's work of creation, while economic conditions that produce unemployment, exploitation, forced migration, homelessness, slave labour, trafficking, and environmental degradation are violations of dignity.

This quotation—taken from a May 30, 2015, meeting between Francis and members of the Science and Life Association—summarizes well the pope's inclusive understanding of human dignity: "When we speak of mankind, we must never forget the various attacks on the sacredness of human life. The plague of abortion is an attack on life. Allowing our brothers and sisters to die on boats in the strait in Sicily is an attack on life. Dying on the job because the minimum safety standards are not respected is an attack on life. Death from malnutrition is an attack on life. Terrorism, war, violence; so is euthanasia. Loving life means always taking care of the other, wanting the best for him, cultivating and respecting her transcendent dignity."

This reference to transcendent dignity is a recurring theme. In his address to the European Parliament in September 2014, Francis explained that it "means appealing to human nature, to our innate capacity to distinguish good from evil, that 'compass' deep within our hearts, which God has impressed upon all creation." This is an implicit rejection of a modern secularized ethos in which dignity loses its moorings in divine transcendence and natural law and becomes an exclusively human attribute of the autonomous rational subject.

There is ambiguity in the Catholic tradition with regard to the dignity of non-human creatures, but Francis is enshrining within official church teaching a holistic understanding of "the intrinsic dignity of the world" (*Laudato Si'* 115). In rejecting the "excessive anthropocentrism" of modernity (LS 116), he is seeking to repair the "web of relationships" in creation, which is modelled upon the subsistent relations of the divine persons (LS 240). In his address to the United Nations in New York in September 2015 he spoke of the "intrinsic value" of all creatures and said that "a true 'right of the environment' does exist."

To appreciate the doctrinal significance of this statement, we might compare Pope Paul VI's 1968 encyclical *Populorum Progressio* with *Laudato Si'*. While the two are similar in their critique of injustice, the former represents "man" as controlling and using nature in a world that is understood primarily in terms of socio-political relationships. Francis earths justice in the deeper and richer soil of the natural environment as God's creation, in a Franciscan–Thomist vision that draws extensively on Orthodox theology and the diverse cultural perspectives offered by bishops' conferences around the world.

Francis's vision of dignity constitutes an inspiring vocation to a life of simplicity and joy nurtured by the beauty of creation, love of neighbour, and the interconnectedness of all life, but there are remaining questions. He repeatedly affirms the dignity of women, but women's extrinsic dignity is still compromised by our exclusion from many offices of Catholic teaching and sacramental ministry on the basis of our sex. The respect for freedom of conscience that is central to human dignity (cf. *Dignitatis Humanae* and *Gaudium et Spes*) is constrained by a celibate male hierarchy claiming authority over the most intimate aspects of women's sexual and reproductive capacities. Church teaching has in recent years affirmed the dignity of homosexual people, but there is considerable ambiguity as to how far this dignity is respected when it comes to sexual love. Unnuanced condemnations of "gender ideology" arguably fail to respect the dignity of transgender and intersex people.

Yet Francis has set the church on a trajectory of change, and he himself acknowledges that this is a messy and conflicted process. He is enriching the historically and culturally contextualized theology of the Second Vatican Council by introducing into it a mystical, sacramental embrace of the dignity of all God's creation. This "integral ecology" has profound implications for the ways in which we express our social, political and personal relationships—our "human ecology" (LS, ch. 4). To speak of the "intrinsic dignity of the world" is to invite a deeper understanding of what it means to be human, living in peace with one another, in solidarity with those who are marginalized, poor and vulnerable, and in relationship with all creatures which participate with us in the mysterious beauty of God's very good creation.

Tina Beattie is professor of Catholic Studies and Director of the Digby Stuart Research Centre for Religion, Society and Human Flourishing and of Catherine of Siena College at the University of Roehampton in London. Her main research interests are in the areas of sacramental theology, Marian theology, gender, and Catholic social teaching.

Discernment

James Martin, SJ

One word that occurs repeatedly in Pope Francis's writings and homilies is "discernment." For Jesuits like the pope, the word is not a generic phrase meaning simply "decision-making" but one with a more specific meaning that is grounded in Jesuit spirituality. Understanding discernment from this perspective is an important key to understanding the pope's approach to making decisions as well as appreciating his advice for both church leaders and the faithful seeking to make good decisions.

Pope Francis's use of discernment is also closely tied to the idea of conscience, a theological tradition highlighted in documents like *Amoris Laetitia*, his apostolic exhortation on the family, particularly when the pope speaks of families (and pastors) facing complicated moral decisions.

In the popular imagination, a "discerning" person is one with good taste or a good eye. They judge well and wisely. For the Jesuit, however, "discernment" means something more. It is the art of prayerful decision-making that employs a set of specific spiritual practices. The Jesuit tradition of discernment is rooted in the *Spiritual Exercises*, the classic manual on prayer written by St. Ignatius Loyola, the sixteenth-century founder of the Jesuit order. In fact, one of the main goals of the *Spiritual Exercises* is to teach people about discernment.

For St. Ignatius discernment means first being aware that God wants us to make good decisions and that God will help us make good decisions, but that we are often moved by competing forces, ones that pull us towards God and those that push us away. Anyone who has ever made an important decision knows this experience. You feel pushed and pulled by a variety of inner forces: selfish versus generous motives, free versus unfree motives, and healthy versus unhealthy motives.

D

So discernment is seeing clearly what those forces are; identifying, weighing and judging them; and finally choosing the path most in line with God's desires for you and for the world. It takes into account the richness and complexity of a person's life and—most importantly— assumes that God is active in the decision-making process itself. As St. Ignatius says in the *Exercises*: "The Creator deals with the creature directly."

Thus, it is not as simple as blindly following a fixed set of rules and regulations. Needless to say, the gospels and church teaching are absolutely essential to form one's conscience, but particularly in times of complexity one must also rely on God's promptings and activity in one's own heart. Often the rules may seem inadequate to a person's lived experience. Likewise, in some situations it may seem that even after one knows and reflects upon the church's laws the best path remains murky.

One can see Pope Francis's reliance on discernment as a pastoral tool perhaps most clearly in *Amoris Laetitia,* which reflected on the proceedings of the Synod of Bishops on the Family, which took place during two sessions in 2014 and 2015. The meeting convened bishops, theologians, and experts from around the world to discuss matters related to family life.

Among the more neuralgic issues raised at the two sessions of the Synod were, first, the reception of Communion by Catholics who were divorced and remarried but had not received annulments of their first marriages and, second, the place of LGBT people in the church. These kinds of pastoral situations, where the church is asked to not only pro- mote adherence to certain rules but also meet people in their complex life situations, are precisely where discernment is most helpful.

Chapter Eight of *Amoris Laetitia,* for example—which is titled "Ac- companying, Discerning and Integrating Weakness"—focuses on, among other things, the situations faced by pastors who wish to accompany people in "irregular" marital situations.

Pope Francis writes:

> If we consider the immense variety of concrete situations such as
> those I have mentioned, it is understandable that neither the Synod
> nor this Exhortation could be expected to provide a new set of gen-
> eral rules, canonical in nature and applicable to all cases. What is
> possible is simply a renewed encouragement to undertake a *respon-*
> *sible personal and pastoral discernment of particular cases*, one which
> would recognize that, since "the degree of responsibility is not equal
> in all cases," the consequences or effects of a rule need not necessarily
> always be the same. (AL 300, emphasis added)

When *Amoris Laetitia* was published, some commentators, including some priests and bishops, expressed surprise, confusion, and even
anger over such passages. (Chapter Eight came under particular scrutiny and criticism.) A few may have been unfamiliar with the concept
of Ignatian discernment, so central to the pope's Jesuit background.
Others seemed to have confused discernment with a kind of "anything
goes" attitude, which would have surprised St. Ignatius Loyola.

So how does one discern?

There are many practices and methods outlined in the *Spiritual*
Exercises. Let me highlight some general ones.

First, you try, as far as possible, to be "indifferent"—that is, free of
anything keeping you from following God's desires. For example, if
you are discerning whether or not to visit a sick friend in the hospital
and you are overly worried about getting sick, you are not sufficiently
"free." Indifferent does not mean that you don't care, nor does it mean
that you are somehow setting aside the rules. Rather, it means that you
are free to follow God's desires in this particular situation.

Second, you ask for God's help, knowing you need that help in choosing the right path. You also need to reflect on the gospels and church
teaching as a way of starting with a good foundation. (That is, you would
never "discern" if you should murder someone.) All this is done in the
context of prayer. But the intellect is fully engaged as well. As Jesuits
like to say, "Trust your heart, but use your head."

Third, you weigh the various "movements" within yourself, to see
which may be coming from God, and which may not be. This is where
St. Ignatius asks us to take seriously the idea that both God and (depend-

ing on what nomenclature you use) the "enemy," the "enemy of human nature," or the "evil spirit" will be pulling you in opposite directions. For someone progressing in the spiritual life, says St. Ignatius, the "good spirit" will bring support, encouragement, and peace of mind. The opposite, however, is true of the "evil spirit," which causes "gnawing anxiety" and throws up "false obstacles" designed to impede one's spiritual progress.

If there still is no clear answer, St. Ignatius suggests other techniques, such as imagining someone in the same situation you are and thinking about what advice you would give him or her. Or imagining what you would want to tell Jesus at the Last Judgment.

Finally, after making a good discernment you will feel a sense of what Ignatius calls "confirmation," or a sense of rightness. You feel in line with God's desires for you because you *are* in line with them. This naturally brings peace.

Overall, discernment recognizes that occasionally rules and traditions cannot tell us which precise path is best. That one size often does not fit all. And that different people may discern in different ways, based on their own consciences.

One of my favourite examples of the ways that discernment can lead people to take different paths, even when the situations seem similar, can be seen with the example of Pope St. John Paul II and Pope Emeritus Benedict XVI.

These two holy men were, at one point in their lives, faced with the same question: should I resign the papacy? Yet the two reached different decisions. John Paul explained that a father can never retire from being the head of a family, and so he chose to continue as pope, even in the face of Parkinson's disease. Benedict said that for the good of the church, he would resign, as he was unable to carry out the many duties of the papacy. Both men discerned; both men listened to their hearts, which spoke to them in the context of their rich and complex lives.

Not every person or pastor will make use of all the traditional practices of discernment as outlined in the *Spiritual Exercises*. But for both individuals and pastors, the overall perspective that discernment offers—that God wants to help us make good decisions, and by paying attention to our hearts we can hear God's voice—is helpful in every case.

Pope Francis's writings speak over and over about discernment—and conscience. They remind us that while rules are important, in pastoral settings something else is needed and relied upon—God's gracious activity within the heart of believers, which helps them to make good, healthy, and life-giving decisions.

Fr. James Martin is a Jesuit priest, editor at large of America *magazine, consultor to the Vatican's Secretariat for Communication, and author of many books, including* The Jesuit Guide to (Almost) Everything, Jesus: A Pilgrimage, My Life with the Saints, Building a Bridge, *and* Seven Last Words.

Ecumenism

Nontando Hadebe

For me, ecumenism is a priority. Today there is an
ecumenism of blood. In some countries they kill Christians
for wearing a cross or having a Bible and before they kill
them they do not ask them whether they are Anglican,
Lutheran, Catholic or Orthodox. Their blood is mixed. To
those who kill, we are Christians. We are united in blood,
even though we have not yet managed to take necessary
steps towards unity between us and perhaps the time has not
yet come. Unity is a gift that we need to ask for. . . . This is
what ecumenism of blood is.
—interview with *La Stampa*, December 2013

Ecumenism is a priority for Pope Francis. He believes the mass killing
of Christians in our time has brought about a new "ecumenism of blood."
Those who kill Christians do not ask to which denomination they belong.

Francis walks in the footsteps of his predecessors who also were committed to ecumenism. He was also active in ecumenical initiatives prior to
his pontificate as archbishop of Buenos Aires, developing what Catholic
website *Crux* reported in December 2016 as a "close friendship" with
Protestant leaders as Cardinal Jorge Bergoglio through an organization
called Renewed Communion of Evangelicals and Catholics in the Spirit.

Surprisingly, Francis has not written an encyclical or apostolic exhortation that systematically lays out his theology and vision of ecumenism,

as was the case with the ecological crisis in his 2015 encyclical *Laudato Si'*. This may be partly due to existing documents by his predecessors on ecumenism, such as the Second Vatican Council decree *Unitatis Redintegratio* and Pope John Paul II's 1995 encyclical *Ut Unum Sint*. Francis has narrated his ecumenical theology, however, in interviews, dialogues, and in encounters with leaders of Orthodox and Protestant churches around the world. Francis's theology of ecumenism can be described as contextual and in continuity with his predecessors. Three descriptions portray his understanding of ecumenism: "ecumenism of blood"; a "spiritual ecumenism" or "ecumenism of prayer" that includes the role of the Holy Spirit; and ecumenism in service of the poor.

As mentioned in the above quotation, Francis uses the phrase "ecumenism of blood" to describe the unintended ecumenism imposed on Christians by their persecutors who are not aware of the differences among them. There are several contexts in which Francis has used this phrase. One notable circumstance was during an ecumenical gathering in St. Peter's Square in 2015. Another was in a May 2015 address to Coptic Orthodox Pope Tawadros II, in which Francis made an appeal for reconciliation between the Coptic and Catholic churches by arguing that already today an "ecumenism of blood unites us."

Pope John Paul II spoke similarly in *Ut Unum Sint*, using the term "martyrology" to describe the communion among Christians through the blood of martyrs. In his encyclical, John Paul said: "In a theocentric vision, we Christians already have a common Martyrology. This also includes the martyrs of our own century, more numerous than one might think, and it shows how, at a profound level, God preserves communion among the baptized in the supreme demand of faith, manifested in the sacrifice of life itself."

Francis's use of the phrases "spiritual ecumenism" and "ecumenism of prayer" indicate an ecumenism that is based on the common baptism that Christians share. For the pope, ecumenism is essentially the work of the Holy Spirit—who sustains diversity, does not impose uniformity, changes hearts, enables Christians to forgive each other for their histories of violence, and transforms Christians of different churches into brothers and sisters.

Francis notably referred to common baptism as a basis of ecumenism during a November 16, 2015, visit to Rome's Evangelical Lutheran Church. In a question-and-answer session during the visit, a Lutheran woman married to a Catholic man told Francis the prohibition on Lutherans receiving Communion in the Catholic Church caused her family sadness.

Francis told the woman that discernment based on the common baptism Lutherans and Catholics share would guide her in finding an appropriate response to the dilemma of taking Communion. "There are explanations, interpretations," the pope said, according to a report of the encounter in *National Catholic Reporter*. "Life is bigger than explanations and interpretations. Always make reference to baptism." The pope continued: " 'One faith, one baptism, one Lord,' Paul tells us. From there, grab hold of the consequences."

Francis took one step further when he and Pope Tawadros signed an April 28, 2017, joint declaration in which they agreed they would no longer hold baptisms for members of one church wishing to join the other. "We, with one mind and heart, will seek sincerely not to repeat the baptism that has been administered in either of our churches for any person who wishes to join the other," the two popes said in the declaration. "This we confess in obedience to the holy Scriptures."

Francis has repeated the emphasis on the Holy Spirit as the agent of ecumenism in many of his statements on ecumenism. When the pope travelled to Istanbul, Turkey, in November 2014 to visit Ecumenical Patriarch Bartholomew, he said the Holy Spirit is not seeking uniformity among the Christian churches but a new sort of diversity. "The more we allow ourselves to be humbly guided by the Spirit of the Lord, the more we will overcome misunderstandings, divisions, and disagreements and be a credible sign of unity and peace," Francis said at Istanbul's Latin-rite church during his visit to Turkey.

In a November 10, 2016, address to the Pontifical Council for Promoting Christian Unity, Francis also said ecumenism does not mean neglecting one's own beliefs. "Christian unity does not lead to a 'reverse ecumenism,' for which one would have to deny their own history of faith," the pope said in that address. "Before seeing what separates us, it is necessary to perceive also in an existential way the wealth of what we have in common, such as the Sacred Scriptures and the great professions of faith of the first ecumenical councils. In this way, we Christians are able to acknowledge we are brothers and sisters who believe in the one Lord and Savior Jesus Christ, committed together to finding the way of obeying today the word of God, who wants us to be united."

A theme that is central in Francis's thought on ecumenism is that ecumenism is not an end in itself but finds its fullest expression in service to the poor. For the pope, the church "cannot be self-centred, revolving around itself."

During Francis's 2014 visit to Turkey, the pope and Patriarch Bartholomew gave public addresses to each other following an Orthodox Divine Liturgy at Istanbul's Church of St. George. Bartholomew asked: "What is the benefit of boasting for what we have received unless these [gifts] translate into life for humanity and our world both today and tomorrow?" Francis said: "The cry of the victims of conflict urges us to move with haste along the path of reconciliation and communion."

Nontando Hadebe was born in Zimbabwe, but resides in South Africa. She has a doctorate in theology from St. Augustine College of South Africa and is now a postdoctoral fellow at the University of South Africa. Raised as a Catholic, her spiritual journey subsequently took her to the Baptist and Anglican/Lutheran churches, before coming back to the Catholic Church.

Embrace

Simcha Fisher

Raise your hand if you remember the first time we met Pope Francis. He stood on the balcony at St. Peter's, his own arm raised in greeting as he stepped out into the night to meet his flock.

Many thought he looked miserable—and stunned. If Catholics were expecting our new papa to match our exuberance, we were disappointed. He had, in fact, already booked his ticket home to Argentina.

But he submitted to the church. He was elected, and there he stood, facing the multitudes as they roared a welcome, his arm raised to greet them; and then he asked for our prayers. Catholics swarmed all over that request, more than making up for his initial reluctance. We clasped our new father to our bosom, enveloping him with love and enthusiasm. Several years into his papacy, he now clearly relishes his role.

That first unequal embrace between papa and church was a good introduction to a pope who frequently uses the word "embrace" when he speaks of spiritual growth; and it endures as a symbol of how he approaches his role, and how he understands the way God and man will be reconciled.

Pope Francis is often chastised for his putative sloppiness, and for what some see as a folksy, imprecise, emotional brand of faith that winks at the law. All those hugs! Who ever was saved because of a hug? Our saviour redeemed us by fulfilling the law on a cross, not by giving us a big hug!

Indeed. Francis knows as well as anyone that an embrace is not a miracle. When he tenderly embraced the tumor-ridden head of the unfortunate pilgrim Vinicio Riva, he did not expect the man to be instantly healed. When we enter into an embrace—either a physical one offered by our fellow Catholics or a spiritual one offered by the church—we are not automatically reconciled to each other or to God, nor do we automatically understand and accept our obligations.

And yet Francis continues to insist on coming together, accompanying, seeking union, and—yes—embracing each other. Is this just naiveté? Does he really think huggy togetherness is an adequate substitute for orthodoxy? Let's look at how he uses that word "embrace."

He frequently references the parable of the Prodigal Son, dwelling on the father's joy as he enfolds his wayward child in his arms, restoring him to the favoured position that he had squandered. The father calls their meeting a resurrection: his son was dead, and now he is alive again. This is an imbalanced embrace, at least at first. The forgiving father is far more enthusiastic than the son, who is humiliated and downcast, hoping only for scraps.

Francis says of this parable that the father makes the son understand that he was always considered a son, in spite of everything. This teaching of Jesus is very important: our condition as children of God is the fruit of the love of the Father's heart; it does not depend on our merits or on our actions, and thus no one can take it away, not even the devil! No one can take this dignity away.

The restorative power of the embrace comes entirely from the love of the father, who represents not only forgiveness but order; whose love restores the son to his place within the orderly structure of his father's household. The son left and behaved lawlessly; he returns to the father purely out of need; the father embraces him with tender love; and the order of the household is restored. Both love and law are entangled in that embrace between unequals.

In *Amoris Laetitia*, an entire passage titled "The Tenderness of an Embrace" also speaks of an imbalanced embrace, comparing the relationship of Christ and the church to a child "sleeping in his mother's arms after being nursed." Francis says: "As the Hebrew word *gamûl* suggests, the infant is now fed and clings to his mother, who takes him to her bosom. There is a closeness that is conscious and not simply biological" (AL 28).

Within that embrace, the mother loves her child all the more because he is helpless and needy. We do not think of a mother primarily as powerful, or as feeding her child merely as an obligation. She willingly cares for the helpless child and feeds him because she loves him; and because she loves him, she uses her strength rightly. Tenderness and obligation are inextricable, both folded into that loving embrace.

Strikingly, in that same passage, the pope draws together the notion of tenderness and the notion of the strictures of law, of obligation. He quotes Hosea: "When Israel was a child, I loved him. . . . I took them up in my arms. . . . I led them with cords of compassion, with the bands of love, and I became to them as one who eases the yoke on their jaws, and I bent down to them and fed them" (Hos 11:1, 3-4).

The pope is speaking not only of tender feelings, but of obligation. When we enter into a loving embrace where there is this imbalance of power, we will be called upon to submit to the law: to receive the love of God and, by that love, to be strengthened to fulfil our obligation to the law. Law and love cannot be disentangled, but love leads us to the law. If an embrace like this is naiveté, then Christ, too, is naive.

This is why Pope Francis so often confounds his critics. On the far left and on the far right, they keep expecting him to say the law doesn't really matter. He is hard to triangulate, since he speaks and dwells in a messy, perilous, imbalanced place, where forgiveness and tenderness are tangled together with obligation.

Francis famously urged his flock to "make a mess." Some took his words and tone as an invitation to flout the law, to follow pure desire. He has caused confusion. He has caused tumult. Also, he has drawn in prodigal sons. He has made the angry, the guilty, the doubtful, the lost think they might return to their father's house again.

And they might. They might not. The embrace is not a miracle. It is an invitation. It is messy and uncertain, but it is most certainly how Christ himself behaved at least some of the time.

Christ is the fulfilment of the law. Christ is love. Christ was that vulnerable child who was nursed by his mother. Christ was tried under law and executed. Christ is the bleeding outcast, the untouchable. Christ is the only one who will embrace us in our misery. Christ is the son of the Father, who asked that the cup might pass from him, but who submitted when he was chosen. Christ sets loving burdens on us. Christ lovingly bears them with us.

It is messy. The embrace is messy. When the law and love meet, one may overwhelm the other. But that perilous moment of contact, between the reluctant and the effusive, between the vulnerable and the strong, between the law and tenderness: that is where we meet God. This is where we meet love forever blessedly entangled with law. If this is naive, then Christ is naive.

Simcha Fisher is a writer and speaker who contributes to several Catholic publications. She is the author of The Sinner's Guide to Natural Family Planning *and blogs at simchafisher.com. She lives in New Hampshire with her husband and ten children.*

Encounter

Archbishop Víctor Manuel Fernández

Francis is constantly inviting us, with both his words and actions, to have an encounter. He has always rejected confrontational discourses, and his ideal is for all of us to come together in an encounter, forming a *polyhedron*, with many facets that create a unified whole with many different aspects. This is a vision of a society in which different people can live together, complement each other, and illuminate each other, although this doesn't exclude arguments or distrust. We can learn something from everyone; no one is useless, no one is expendable. Someone on the periphery sees things that I don't see, because he or she has a perspective that I don't have and observes reality from a different position. My encounter with that person involves recognizing his or her value as a person, and in this way, gathering something from their experience and perspective.

This does not mean losing my identity, because my identity is also part of the polyhedron; it is my contribution, my gift to others. If there are no clear identities, there is no conflict, but neither is there a real encounter; it is all an empty shell. For this reason, Francis insists that it is not healthy to flee from conflicts or to ignore them. We must accept them and suffer them through to the end, not hide them. But we must always do this with the ideal of resolving them, of harmonizing the differences. From two different things can come a synthesis that is better than and improves upon both, although both also have to renounce something. We must always aim for something new, in which violent tensions and selfish interests are overcome.

The construction of this "unity in diversity" or "reconciled diversity" is also expressed in Francis's gestures of *rapprochement* with other religions and other churches. For the same reason, he does not object to there being people in the church who criticize his decisions harshly. There is a place for the other, for what is different.

But, what is added when Francis uses the expression, "culture of encounter"? The word "culture" refers to something that has penetrated to the heart of a people. When something becomes culture, it has become a shared "passion," and in the end, a lifestyle that characterizes that human group. It means that, as a people, we are passionate about seeking points in common, building bridges, creating a project that includes us all. The people as a whole are the subject of culture, not a group of a select few.

This encounter requires hard work. The easiest thing would be to limit freedoms and differences with a bit of cunning and resources. That peace would be superficial and fragile. Integration is much slower and more difficult, but it is the guarantee of real and solid peace. Can that be achieved by bringing together only the beautiful people, the saints, the pure? Francis replies, "Even people who can be considered dubious on account of their errors have something to offer which must not be overlooked" (*Evangelii Gaudium* 236). Nor can we settle for a peace that is achieved by silencing the demands of social justice or by keeping these concerns from being voiced publicly, because it is not a matter of "creating a consensus on paper or a transient peace for a contented minority" (EG 218), nor a project to fabricate a peace "drawn up by a few for the few" (EG 239).

The goal is to create *processes* of encounter that will build up a people enriched by their differences. These processes must also be oriented towards those who are "disposable," the forgotten, and the invisible, to the point of touching their wounded flesh. Some opponents go so far as to say that this insistence of Francis on including the poor and the weak is proper to a populist, and that it leads to the deterioration of the culture of work. Nonetheless, he upholds that "welfare projects, which meet certain urgent needs, should be considered merely temporary responses" (EG 202). He also explains that he is not simply talking about giving food or money, but "above all employment, for it is through free, creative, participatory and mutually supportive labour that human beings express and enhance the dignity of their lives" (EG 192). Clearly, when he speaks of incorporating the lives of the poor in a true social encounter, he is asking that everyone have real opportunities to rise to a better life thanks to personal effort and development. How can we construct a precious polyhedron if we don't make every person's abilities flourish?

In a message from Francis to the people of Argentina (September 30, 2016), he spoke again about the culture of encounter. There, he made a clarification: this encounter means that each person "should be able to express himself peacefully, without being insulted, condemned, attacked, or cast to one side." That is to say, anyone must be able to express a different opinion, offer a nuanced view, or set forth a different aspect of a situation without having a waterfall of insults and suspicions rain down on them. There are many subtle ways of silencing those who are different. When that happens, an encounter becomes impossible. An authentic encounter presupposes recognizing the other's right to be himself and to be different. For this reason, what Francis proposes is a "cultural covenant": a decision and agreement in favour of respect, tolerance and dialogue among different parties, which establishes the foundation for political agreement. This means that those involved have learned to recognize the other *as other*: each with his or her own way of seeing life, of going forward, of expressing opinions, of feeling, and of dreaming.

Beneath all that has been said lies a common root: the capacity to appreciate, with profound conviction, *the great worth of a human being*, always and in any circumstance. This is important because sometimes it seems like some people are worth more than others, that some are more human than others. Nonetheless, as Francis says, "the mere fact that some people are born in places with fewer resources or less development does not justify the fact that they are living with less dignity" (EG 190). This is precisely the deepest foundation of an authentic culture of encounter: the other person has rights, but he has them not due to the economic value of what he can do, but rather due to the infinite value of his or her human dignity, which transcends any circumstance or any result. A person's rights do not have their origin in what he or she has inherited from his family, in bearing a certain last name, in having certain abilities, and not even in the formation he has received. A person's value lies in the inviolable dignity that he or she possesses as a human being. If this principle were forgotten, as Francis says, there would be no meaning in "an investment in efforts to help *the slow, the weak, or the less talented to find opportunities in life*" (EG 209).

This warns us of a very subtle deception. Some say that, in the end, what is important is that there be equal opportunities for all; that is to say, the same *starting point* for all. Afterwards, everything depends on the effort of each person. That could seem correct. But the reality is that whoever is less talented or is weaker, whether by nature or by the context in which they happen to live, will never have equal opportunities. They need to be, and should be, given special help on their path through life so that they may give the best of themselves, even accepting that this may not be the most efficient course of action. Because what matters is that they develop all of their human potential, beyond the economic value of what they might be able to produce. Their immense dignity demands it. Only when we recognize this is true encounter possible, and in this way, working together, we can build bit by bit that precious polyhedron made of many facets.

Archbishop Víctor Manuel Fernández is the rector of the Pontifical Catholic University of Argentina. A noted theologian, he is a former president of the Argentine Theology Society and was elevated to the dignity of archbishop by Pope Francis in May 2013.

Episcopal accountability

Katie Grimes

The cause of accountability is unfinished business in the Catholic Church, especially with respect to the clergy sex abuse crisis. Incredibly, more than fifteen years after the news of systemic cover-up broke in the United States, many survivors are still seeking justice—or at least the assurance that what happened to them will not happen to others.

When Francis was elected to papal office in 2013, many Catholics hoped that this would all change. Even more than his predecessors, Francis has cultivated an intensely pastoral approach to the priesthood. And who better to protect God's sheep than a shepherd?

But for many survivors and their allies, these hopes have soured. As clergy sex abuse survivor and activist Marie Collins explained in the *National Catholic Reporter* after announcing her 2017 resignation from Pope Francis's Pontifical Commission for the Protection of Minors, despite the fact that Francis "does at heart understand the horror of abuse and the need for those who would hurt minors to be stopped," other high-ranking church officials nonetheless have refused "to implement the recommendations of the commission."

We may feel tempted to blame Francis for this failure. But rather than asking what Francis ought to do to hold abusers accountable, we ought to ask why survivors of clergy sexual abuse have so far been unable to do so. Composed partially of lay people barred from participating in church governance, the pontifical commission can only make suggestions; it cannot issue commands. Put another way, the commission failed not because of what certain Vatican officials refused to do, but because of what it could not make them do. Focusing on Francis, though understandable, only distracts us from the root cause of the commission's failure: its lack of power, as described by Paul Vallely in his book *Untying the Knots: The Struggle for the Soul of Catholicism*.

Indeed, no one can hold another person accountable unless she has the power to do so. And in the hierarchical Catholic Church, power flows downwards much more easily than it surges upwards, as *Lumen Gentium* describes. For this reason, survivors of clergy sexual abuse must convince those they cannot compel—the bishops—to change the way they exercise their power over the priests below them. No wonder accountability has so far proven elusive.

In response to these failures, we may also wish that more bishops and Vatican officials would follow more closely in Francis's pastoral footsteps. Surely wounded sheep need better shepherds. But Francis's pastoral approach to priestly office paradoxically enables the clerical intransigence it aims to disrupt. This claim initially may seem unfair. After all, Francis's pastoral interpretation of papal power seemingly epitomizes the Second Vatican Council's contention that "bishops . . . with priests and deacons as helpers, took on the ministry to the community" and in so doing "presid[e] in God's place [as shepherds] over the flock" (*Lumen Gentium* 20). For the Second Vatican Council as for Francis, the bishops do not simply serve the church by governing it; they govern the church by serving it, that is, they follow in "the example of the Good Shepherd," Jesus Christ (LG 27).

But this understanding of the priesthood appears feasible only because the word "service" has acquired a meaning that bears very little in common with true servitude. Today, for example, we consider volunteer work and the pursuit of elected office as forms of "service." But the New Testament perceives "service" as closely related to and sometimes indistinguishable from slavery. Plus, the word translated as "service" in English-speaking renditions of the New Testament sometimes comes from the Greek word, *doulos*, which referred to slaves and slavery, not servants and service, as described by Jennifer A. Glancy in her 2011 book *Slavery as a Moral Problem: In the Early Church and Today*. Reflecting this similarity, the English word "service" derives from the Latin word for slave, *servus*.

Even when priests and bishops act as slaves or servants to God, they do not act as slaves or servants to lay people. For example, while priests and bishops are endowed with the power to govern others, slaves are denied the right to act as rulers even of themselves. Enslaved people exercise power only in the name of and with the permission of their master. In contrast, priests and bishops neither require nor seek the consent of laity; they do not take orders from them. And, although servants possess more rights than slaves, they remain subordinates to their master in a way priests and bishops never have been to the laity.

Could it be otherwise? Church tradition also positions priests as *presbyteroi*, or elders, and bishops as *episkopoi*, or overseers. Rather than modes of service, these capacities conflict with it. Slavery infantilizes its victims: even when they are very old, enslaved people are denied the honour ordinarily accorded to elders. And while overseers are sometimes also enslaved, they are slaves to their masters, not those they oversee. Bishops can be overseers of the laity or they can be servants to them, but they cannot be both.

In truth, priests and bishops could act as slaves or servants to the laity only if the laity were empowered to act as masters over them. And if lay people were positioned as masters of priests and bishops, they would have no problem holding sexually abusive clergymen accountable.

But rather than masters of clergymen, the laity are their sheep. And sheep are servants to their shepherd much more than they are served by him. While sheep can be made to follow their shepherds, they can never lead them. Sheep can induce their shepherd to chase them down if they go astray, but they cannot hold their shepherd accountable when he steps out of line. And like slaves and servants who are rendered artificially dependent on their masters, sheep live through and because of the benevolence of their shepherd.

Especially in the wake of the sex abuse crisis, theologies of priestly service have obscured the perils and powerlessness of sheeplike dependence on even good shepherds like Francis. As long as they are sheep, lay Catholics will never be able to protect themselves against wolves in shepherds' clothing. More than simply unable to hold church officials accountable, lay Catholics will remain at their mercy.

Katie Grimes is an assistant professor of theological ethics at Villanova University. Her research focuses on anti-blackness and the Catholic Church.

Family

Julie Hanlon Rubio

Pope Francis is beloved by many because he locates the heart of Christian faith in justice and care for the most vulnerable, especially the very poor and the earth itself. In both his actions and his public statements, his focus on social justice has been extraordinarily consistent and powerful.

Yet he chose to utilize the powerful instrument of a synod—a gathering of the world's bishops designed to offer guidance to the pope on a pressing issue—to bring attention not to poverty or environmental destruction but to the family. The synod was announced early in his papacy and took place in 2014 and 2015. A final document was produced, but Pope Francis followed up in 2016 with his own document on the family: *Amoris Laetitia* (The Joy of Love).

The pope knew that if he wanted the church to truly be a "field hospital," he would have to talk about family. Family is where people are hurting, ashamed, and broken. Often, it is the church teachings on family issues that alienate people. If the church is to truly welcome people and be a greater force for good in the world, conversations about family cannot be avoided.

But because he wanted the church to change, Pope Francis had to talk about family in a different way. This difference was on display in his visit to the United States in 2015. In his homily for the US bishops, he used family imagery to speak about the church, saying "it is important that the church in the United States also be a humble home, a family fire which attracts men and women through the attractive light and warmth of love."

According to Francis, both the church and families should be known by their warmth, humility, and love. This vision of church and family is the main thing Francis wants to communicate. Five other aspects of the pope's way of talking about family flow from this central vision.

1. Unlike previous popes, who most often spoke of "the family," Francis often uses "family" or "families." This subtle shift in language is indicative of a more inclusive vision. Rather than holding up the Holy Family as perfect, Francis stresses their struggles as poor refugees fleeing violence while facing an unexpected pregnancy (AL 30).

   Importantly, Francis acknowledges that partial realizations of the ideal (e.g., cohabiting couples, single-parent households, remarried couples) can be valuable, if not all that we would hope for. Today, social forces (like poverty and migration) make it more difficult to hold families together. Yet "every family, despite its weaknesses, can become a light in the darkness of the world" (AL 66).

2. Early in *Amoris Laetitia*, Pope Francis claims: "the Bible is full of families, births, love stories and family crises" (AL 8). Along with Cardinal Walter Kasper (who presented his idea of the "Gospel of the family," at the Vatican prior to the synod, and later published a small book with the same title), Francis insists on the centrality and messiness of family life in scripture. The claim perhaps overlooks the lack of attention to families in the New Testament, not to mention Jesus' hard sayings about family. Still, the basic insight that God is love so God is present even in the most imperfect of families, is both traditional and borne out in contemporary experience. Francis tries to avoid abstraction by speaking of and to "real families" (AL 36). Rather than stressing doctrine and bemoaning the decline of family values, he recognizes that "most people do value family relationships that are permanent and marked by mutual respect" and, like the families whose stories are told in the Bible, they have complicated lives marked by grace (AL 38).

3. Many Catholic documents include discussion of challenges to the family. The USCCB's pastoral letter, *Marriage: Life and Love in the Divine Plan* (2009), identifies four: same-sex unions, contraception, divorce, and cohabitation. Pope Francis shares the bishops'

concern about the fragility of marriage, but he focuses on different challenges.

His speech to Congress during his visit to the United States revealed his priorities. Though he was on his way to the World Meeting of Families in Philadelphia and in the middle of a synod, he said little about family. After discussing political divisions, immigration, the death penalty, poverty, the environment, and war, the pope expressed concern for "the family, which is threatened, perhaps as never before, from within and without." Francis then surprised his audience by speaking not of same-sex unions or contraception but of vulnerable young people "trapped in a hopeless maze of violence, abuse, and despair." He challenges traditional Catholics by identifying injustice as the primary threat to family values.

4. Francis often links home and family. In his encyclical on the environment, the earth is called "our common home." Francis uses imagery borrowed from St. Francis of Assisi ("Brother Sun" and "Sister Moon," LS 87) to make the environmental crisis personal. He suggests that because we are all connected in "one single human family" (LS 52), we have to think about the long-term implications of the way we live. We have a real responsibility of "intergenerational solidarity" to "future generations" (LS 159). Because "everything is interconnected" (LS 240), it only makes sense to think about families and ecology together.

5. Finally, though Francis is sometimes accused of diluting Catholic teaching on family, his speeches and writings reveal his consistent efforts to lift up a compelling vision of family in a world where many question its relevance. In the final section of *Amoris Laetitia*, he offers a spirituality of marriage and family. Marriage involves the challenge of loving another person forever, cultivating love over time so that we may grow old together. Families are "the nearest 'hospital,'" a chance to take part in "God's dream . . . of building a world in which no one will feel alone" (AL 319–21). Yet, like the church, instead of remaining closed within themselves, they become more themselves by "going forth," "caring for others," and "transforming the world" (AL 324). If cultural norms about family stress success for parents and kids, Francis places his hope in families who will strive to love each other forever and bring their love to the world.

In talking about "family" as a place of warmth and love, identifying serious challenges, and presenting an inclusive vision focused on love and social justice, Pope Francis has made it possible for many more people to see their realities and their hopes in the church's ideals and to envision the church as more like a home.

Julie Hanlon Rubio is Professor of Christian ethics at St. Louis University. Her most recent book is Reading, Living, Praying Pope Francis's The Joy of Love: A Faith Formation Guide *(Liturgical Press).*

Field hospital

Cardinal Blase Cupich

Jorge Bergoglio needed just a few minutes to reorient radically the Catholic Church. In the days leading up to a conclave, cardinals deliver addresses designed to help their brothers discern where the Spirit is calling the church. Some go longer, some shorter. In his 2013 pre-conclave intervention, Bergoglio didn't waste his time.

"In Revelation," the soon-to-be-pope explained, "Jesus says that he is at the door and knocks." The idea, he continued, is that Jesus is knocking from outside the door. But Bergoglio inverted the image, and according to notes he later gave to Cardinal Jaime Ortega, asked his brother cardinals, and indeed the whole church, to consider "the times in which Jesus knocks from within so that we will let him come out." When the church keeps Christ to herself and doesn't let him out, he continued, it becomes "self-referential—and then gets sick." To avoid this, according to Bergoglio, the church must go out of itself to the peripheries, to minister to the needy.

This is evangelization. This is the mission entrusted to the church by Jesus Christ—and it was precisely in this moment that he foreshadowed his programme for the Catholic Church as a "field hospital" for the wounded, a profound, indeed stunning image he would deliver in a surprise interview with Jesuit Fr. Antonio Spadaro soon after he became pope.

By calling the church a "field hospital," Pope Francis calls us to radically rethink ecclesial life. He is challenging all of us to give priority to the wounded. That means placing the needs of others before our own. The "field hospital church" is the antithesis of the "self-referential church." It is a term that triggers the imagination, forcing us to rethink our identity, mission, and our life together as disciples of Jesus Christ.

Medics are useless if the wounded cannot reach them. Those who have the bandages go to those with the wounds. They don't sit back in their offices waiting for the needy to come to them. The field hospital marshals all its institutional resources in order to serve those who most need help now.

Of course one cannot prioritize the needy without understanding their sufferings and challenges. This entails listening. We begin with a question: "How can we help?" Then they tell us where it hurts. This requires patience, docility and openness to learning about how best to serve them in the particular circumstances and relationships that mark their lives. This is neither the place nor the time for pre-diagnoses in the form of prejudgments or predeterminations. In the language of spiritual direction, we call that discernment. Discernment is a word that reminds us to seek what is possible, what is of value, what is working in the person that will help reintegrate him or her back into society.

Of course, there is a risk in going out into the field of battle, of moving out of one's comfort zone and the security of one's experience. Pope Francis speaks about our need to leave the safety of the sacristy for the mess of being with the needy. Pastors have to be unafraid to get mud on their shoes. They have to be willing to make mistakes that come from learning from the wounded and trying new treatments. How many cures have been discovered in the urgency of combat? Improvisation can lead to creative solutions.

The medicine in this field hospital has a name. It's called mercy. The medicine of mercy is ever adaptable to meet the present need; it is available to all and requires no prescription. Mercy isn't mercy if it resides at the end of an obstacle course, or has to compete with power, or is reserved for the wounds of a few, or—worse—requires a certain level of health before being applied. Recall the conversation Francis had with Vatican journalist Andrea Tornielli, published as *The Name of God Is Mercy*, where the pope reminds us that "'mercy' derives from *misericordis*, which means opening one's heart to wretchedness." Mercy is not repulsed by the infected sore, for it is made for it.

Bringing the medicine of mercy to the world is the most effective way for the disciples of Jesus to recapture the joy of the Gospel. The field hospital heals the healers as well. Something transformative happens to them as they work together to serve the needy. They gain a fresh sense of purpose, hope, and joy about life as they discover new ways of healing.

So it goes with the church. When the church becomes a field hospital it can radically change the way we view our community life. Instead of being defined as a group of people that live in the same neighbourhood, have a common ethnic heritage or social status, regularly go to Mass, or are the registered parishioners, we understand ourselves as those who take up the work of healing by sharing in the sufferings of others. We are a community that taps into and shares our talents to find creative ways to help those most in need. We already know this about ourselves, as Jesus gave us this truth at the very start of his ministry when he announced that he was sent "to bring glad tidings to the poor . . . sent . . . to proclaim liberty to captives and recovery of sight to the blind, to let the oppressed go free, and to proclaim a year acceptable to the Lord" (Luke 4:18-19).

That is Christ's challenge for the church today: to be a field hospital for the needy. To bring those glad tidings, not to sit back and wait for those who need them to ask. To go out, to travel to the peripheries where the oppressed reside. To be with the wounded on the field of battle. This is what is acceptable to the Lord. It is radical. Mercy always is. And as Pope Francis continues to remind us of this truth, he takes us back to our Christian roots, helping us realize that it has been with us all along.

Cardinal Blase Cupich is the archbishop of Chicago, Illinois. He previously served as the head of the dioceses of Spokane, Washington, and Rapid City, South Dakota.

Flesh

Dario E. Viganò

"Jesus Christ did not save us with an idea, or an intellectual programme. He saved us with his flesh, with the concreteness of the flesh. He lowered himself, became man, and was made flesh until the end," Pope Francis said at a morning Mass in June 2013. The church, an expert in humanity, believes in Christ who has come in human flesh and therefore continues to invite us to serve the human person, to love the human person, to believe in the human person, because in the flesh of every woman and every man, exhausted by the journey of life, we know that we are touching the flesh of our Lord.

"And the Word became flesh" (John 1:14). This is the heart of the Christian *kerygma*, the proclamation of the incarnation of the only-begotten Son of God who truly became a human person without truly ceasing to be God. In the Bible, the word *flesh* (*sarx* in Greek, the language of the gospels, and *bāśār* in Hebrew) does not refer simply to the human body or to the physical part of the person, as though a person could be divided in such a dichotomous way. Rather, it refers to the person as spirit, soul, and body united in space and time. The *Catechism of the Catholic Church* points to this when it teaches that "Because 'human nature was assumed, not absorbed,' in the mysterious union of the Incarnation, the Church was led over the course of centuries to confess the full reality of Christ's human soul, with its operations of intellect and will, and of his human body." The catechism also notes how Christ's human nature, too, belongs to the divine person of the Son of God, who assumed it. "In his soul as in his body, Christ thus expresses humanly the divine ways of the Trinity: 'The Son of God . . . worked with human hands; he thought with a human mind. He acted with a human will, and with a human heart he loved,'" says the catechism, quoting *Gaudium et Spes* (22).

The flesh of Christ, then, makes God's "dream" for humanity possible. In fact, "the completion of Christ's mission comes when he speaks, in his very body, the full and final word of love, by handing himself over into the hands of humanity," as Jesuit Fr. Marko Rupnik has written.

Christianity inverts the paradigm established in Greek thought of the relationship between humanity and divinity, a paradigm that has also too often marked the history and the experience of the Christian faith. Before Christianity, humanity was understood to have to rely on its own strengths—emotional, intellectual, and spiritual—in its attempts to participate in divine life, a life that remained inaccessible because of the experience of death, which stood like a tombstone blocking the path to the fulfilment of the human desire for the infinite. Now, with the incarnation of Christ, God takes on our flesh, experiencing even the limits of death so that "if we have died with him, we shall also live with him" (2 Tim 2:11).

For the disciple, the flesh of humanity is no longer the element that must be overcome in order to reach God, as though the spiritual is opposed to the physical. The flesh, rather, is revealed as the means by which we can experience the infinite love of God who, in his mercy, comes to meet us, to remind us of our lost dignity, and to make us participants in the love of the Trinity.

"Whoever eats my flesh and drinks my blood has eternal life, and I will raise him on the last day. . . . Whoever eats my flesh and drinks my blood remains in me and I in him" (John 6:54, 56). Jesus breaks open a new horizon of our existence, enabling us to welcome his life in us and to live according to his logic of love and self-giving. All of this becomes possible, by the power of the incarnation, in and through our flesh, which can be given up for the people we encounter in our own lives. The life of Christ, brought to completion in the offering of his own flesh for our salvation, invites and enables us to live in this dynamic of life received and offered so that a spark of eternal Trinitarian love shines in us.

In this sense, the flesh is an urgent calling to and constant verification of our being disciples of Christ. Pope Francis wrote in his message for the first World Day of the Poor:

If we truly wish to encounter Christ, we have to touch his body in the suffering bodies of the poor, as a response to the sacramental communion bestowed in the Eucharist. The Body of Christ, broken in the sacred liturgy, can be seen, through charity and sharing, in the faces and people of the most vulnerable of our brothers and sisters. St. John Chrysostom's admonition remains ever timely: "If you want to honour the body of Christ, do not scorn it when it is naked; do not honour the Eucharistic Christ with silk vestments, and then, leaving the church, neglect the other Christ suffering from cold and nakedness."

In the flesh of every man and every woman there lies hidden the intimate and profound secret of the passion of the Father for each of us. This is why we are called to live every relationship in the way of God, according to the logic of the kingdom and not according to the worldly logic of dominance and power. Experiencing God's way of love in our very flesh, we are able to do everything we do through him, with him and in him, making our very life a liturgy.

Time and again Pope Francis has emphasized how the incarnation and our response to it involves the concreteness of living and the experience of other people that we have through our bodies, in the flesh. "The Word became flesh, he did not become an idea: he became flesh," the pope noted during a homily at one of his morning Masses in April 2017. He continued by insisting that when we recite the Creed what we say is "concrete": " 'I believe in God the Father, creator of heaven and earth; I believe in Jesus Christ, who was born, who died. . . .' They are all concrete things. The Creed does not say: 'I believe that I must do this, that I must do that'. . . . No! They are concrete things." This "concreteness of faith" leads "to frankness, to witnessing to the point of martyrdom, which is contrary to compromises or the idealization of faith."

The Holy Father speaks of a concrete love, which has its source in the incarnation. We can therefore never allow our understanding of the incarnation to fall into the seductive mechanicalism of an intellectualized, ideologized, and abstract Christianity that has nothing to do with human experience, marked as it is by weakness and death. The pope has preached that the model and criteria of Christian love is not the kind of love portrayed in a soap opera or novel, and not even the theoretical love of philosophers, but is rather the incarnation of the Word. The term "flesh" therefore points to the mystery of the cross, to the crucified and risen One. As the Apostle Paul affirms: "For our sake he made him to be sin who did not know sin, so that we might become the righteousness of God in him" (2 Cor 5:21).

Msgr. Dario Edoardo Viganò is prefect of the Vatican's Secretariat for Communication.

Gossip

Kaya Oakes

Most of us know on an intrinsic level that gossip is bad for us. While flipping through a tabloid at the dentist's office feels innocuous, we excuse bad-mouthing people behind their backs as a temporary stress release. But when gossip becomes a habit and when we use it to manipulate others, it leaves a bad taste in our mouths, like gobbling down a greasy fast-food meal only to regret it soon after.

For Pope Francis, however, gossip is something worse than a fleeting, guilty pleasure. Francis tells us repeatedly that gossip is divisive at its root, and as a result gossip may in fact be a tool of the devil. Speaking to a group of bishops of mission territories in September 2016, the pope described gossip as "idle chatter that divides," and even as "a habit of terrorism." Gossip, he said, is a bomb thrown "in order to destroy both the local church and the universal one."

Anyone who's been involved in parish work knows how this operates in a local church. A new pastor comes in and changes things. People talk. A new music director tosses out beloved hymns. People talk. A new parishioner arrives and tries to start a group for women, LGBT people, lapsed Catholics, teens. People talk. A bishop orders a parish to change something in the liturgy. People talk. Chatter and complaint are human nature, and no one is innocent of this. At some basic level, gossip is a search for a shared sense of the truth.

But where this chatter turns into what the pope calls "a weapon of the devil" is when it amplifies and finds a target. At a local church, this can lead to a kind of modern-day shunning, one in which individuals are iced out, ignored, turned down for committee work, or made to feel so uncomfortable that they leave. Priests are not innocent of this; they too can fall into the habit of grousing about parishioners and one another, and especially about their bishops. But all of these patterns begin in gossip. A rumour begins with an individual who hears something. Like the childhood game of telephone, as it passes from one person to another it becomes distorted and amplified to the point that the true story is lost. The demonic aspect of this pattern is about the power to control the narrative. The truth is stolen from the individual being gossiped about—and given over to the gossipers.

This is only amplified in our age of social media, where gossip runs rampant. One needs to only briefly think about the conspiracy theories and rumours that flew back and forth across Twitter and Facebook during the last US presidential election. Or one might even recall some of the online commentary on the pope's own writings, the gossip that bubbled up during the 2015 Synod of Bishops and during Francis's election, the endless gossip mill of the Catholic blogosphere, or the "two popes" theory that insists Pope Benedict XVI is still in control of the church.

Gossip is inherent to communication in the digital age, and it bleeds into coverage of the Vatican. This is nothing new: Xavier Rynne, the pseudonym of Redemptorist priest Francis X. Murphy, wrote chatty, gossipy columns about the Second Vatican Council for *The New Yorker*. The Vatican is a place of rumour and intrigue, and both are hard to resist, which may be why Francis, who spent less time in Rome than his predecessor before being elected pope, speaks out so harshly about gossip.

But the pope's message about the danger of gossip is not exclusive to church leaders or even to Catholics. The pope reiterated it when he told a group of Italian journalists in September 2016 that rumour-mongering is an example of "terrorism, of how you can kill a person with your tongue." This, he added, "is even more true for journalists because their voice can reach everyone and this is a very powerful weapon," especially in an age of twenty-four-hour news cycles that allow little time for fact-checking. Journalism based on rumours, he said, can easily be used as a "weapon of destruction against persons and even entire peoples." Yet again, it is hard to hear the pope's words and not think of our online lives, where we are bombarded with media around the clock, much of it in the form of "fake news." For journalists such as myself, resisting the urge to click, retweet, or circulate poorly sourced stories is challenging under the relentless pressure to produce fresh content. But the pope is correct: these stories can do real damage. It's worth remembering that when we're rushing towards a deadline.

To gossip is to speak without thinking, write without fact-checking, or tweet without sourcing. Gossip is instant gratification, and, as with so many other kinds of instant gratification, the after-effects are something we rarely consider in the moment. As with so many things the pope says that lead to a feeling of discomfort, his words about gossip sting because so many of us indulge in it. In this historical epoch when gossip can destroy lives in an instant, opting not to participate in it is countercultural. What Pope Francis instead challenges us to do is to seek something more difficult. It's called truth.

Kaya Oakes is the author of four books, most recently including The Nones Are Alright. *A senior correspondent at* Religion Dispatches *and a contributing writer at* America *magazine, she teaches writing at the University of California, Berkeley.*

Grandparents

Bill Dodds

It's great for us grandparents to get a papal pat on the back from Pope Francis.

We tend not to give ourselves one, and not just because of a touch of arthritis in an elbow or a bit of bursitis in a shoulder. It's more a feeling of "I used to do more, and what I'm doing now doesn't seem like much." No, no, no, says the Holy Father who, in many ways, can be the "Holy Grandfather." He's not a grandpa but—ah, when he starts reminiscing about his Grandma Rosa. It's clear he knows what he's talking about when it comes to the impact a member of the oldest generation can have on the heart, the mind, and the soul of a member of the youngest. On a little boy in Buenos Aires, Argentina.

And, from what he tells us, it is clear that one grandmother's impact is being felt in the Catholic Church in the twenty-first century. Through that "little boy," it's resounding worldwide. Four examples:

- "The words of grandparents contain something special for young people. And they know it. The words that my grandmother gave me in writing the day of my priestly ordination I still carry with me, always, in the breviary. And I read them often and they do me good."

- "We pray for our grandfathers, our grandmothers, who so often play a heroic role in the transmission of the faith in times of persecution. When mum and dad weren't home or when they had strange ideas, which the politics of the time taught them, it was the grandmothers who passed on the faith."

- "One of the most beautiful things in life, in the family, in our lives, is caressing a child and letting yourself be caressed by a grandfather or a grandmother."

- "Grandparents are a treasure. Often old age isn't pretty, right? There is sickness and all that, but the wisdom our grandparents have is something we must welcome as an inheritance."

But, Pope Francis points out, it isn't just grandparents but all elders who are offered this vocation that, literally, takes decades of preparation. Among other things, he has said:

- "The elderly are those who transmit history to us, who transmit doctrine, who transmit the faith and give it to us as an inheritance."

- "It is also important to promote the bond between generations. The future of a people requires the encounter between young and old: the young people are the vitality of a people 'on the way' and the elderly reinforce this vitality with memory and wisdom."

- "The church regards the elderly with affection, gratitude, and high esteem. They are an essential part of the Christian community and of society: in particular they represent the roots and the memory of a people. You are an important presence, because your experience is a precious treasure, which is essential if we would look to the future with hope and responsibility. Your maturity and wisdom, accumulated over the years, can help younger people in search of their own way, supporting them on the path of growth and openness to the future."

- "In a world like this, in which strength and appearance are often mythologized, your mission is to bear witness to the values that really matter and that endure forever because they are engraved on the heart of every human being and guaranteed by the Word of God. Precisely as people in the so-called 'third age,' you, or rather we—because I too am one of them—we are called to work for the development of the culture of life, witnessing that every season of life is a gift from God and has its own beauty and its importance, though marked by fragility."

I think of my own grandchildren's grandma—my wife, Monica—who died of uterine cancer in early 2013 at the age of sixty. About her final year when all the family, including a four-year-old girl and seven-year-old boy, knew what was happening. What was that grandma's legacy? What was those children's inheritance? Love.

Time and time again, compressed into twelve short months, they shared a love, they strengthened a bond that—thanks to the communion of saints—hasn't ended. And never will. And now part of my vocation isn't simply that of memory-keeper, but memory-sharer. It's pulling out photos or looking at videos with them that show that happy, holy, little "trinity" having the kind of fun that only those two generations can have. It's telling my stories and listening to theirs. It's being a grandpa for them and with them, because that God-given role is at the core of my vocation at this point in my life.

Yes, I used to do more but, I'm certain, nothing that was more important.

Bill Dodds and his late wife, Monica, were the founders of the Friends of St. John the Caregiver (FSJC.org), an international Catholic organization that promotes care for family caregivers.

Hagan lío!

Manuel Dorantes

Hagan lío! is a very Argentine instruction to "shake things up." It's a call to action, an invitation to not remain still or silent, especially after someone has caused you harm. It's a much more gracious version of an even more commonly used phrase among Argentinians, especially young ones. But that other one is rather vulgar and, though common, would not be an appropriate phrase for a pope—even an Argentinian one who talks like ordinary people. (If you would like to know the vulgar version, consult your nearest Argentinian.)

Just four months into his pontificate, Pope Francis first issued the instruction at a meeting with young Argentinians during World Youth Day 2013 in Rio de Janeiro, Brazil. "What do I expect as a consequence of World Youth Day?" he asked them in the city's cathedral. "I expect *lío*. We know there will be *lío* inside this building, we know there will be *lío* in Rio, but I want you to shake things up in the dioceses, I want the dioceses to go outside of themselves, I want the church to go out into the streets, I want us to defend ourselves against everything that is worldliness, everything that means remaining still, everything that means comfort, every form of clericalism, everything that means being locked up inside ourselves, inside our parishes, inside our schools!"

When those young Argentinians heard the phrase they roared with approval. They knew exactly what he meant. He wanted them to shake things up by not remaining passive spectators in the lives of their local churches and communities. Since that first encounter in Rio he has used the phrase exclusively when he has met with young people. He did it in Brazil, in Paraguay, most recently during World Youth Day 2016 in Poland, and he has used it often when meeting young people in Rome. That little three-letter word has become *the* battle call of Pope Francis to the youth of our time.

Today's young people have grown up overwhelmed by the latest in personal technology. There are many blessings of this new interconnectedness, but negative impacts too: isolation, narcissism, and a certain indifference to anyone outside a person's bubble. The last is most concerning to the Holy Father. Many young people have been anaesthetized by the smartphone, the trending app, or the latest video game. While people in their local communities suffer and cry out for help and relationship, these young victims of consumerism have become firmly attached to their sofas, unable to enter into a personal relationship, much less to feel their brother's or sister's pain. They are no longer the protagonists of their lives but passive spectators. Their lives pass them by, devoid of purpose.

Saint Augustine's classical definition of sin is quite applicable to this phenomenon: *incurvatus in se*, or "curved into oneself." So defined, sin breaks the bonds of relationship: it isolates us; it makes us indifferent. When we are disconnected from the reality around us because we are connected to our machines, we have curved into ourselves; sin has conquered us. When the world of digital relationships takes precedence over real relationships, we have become curved into ourselves.

Radical individualism rooted in indifference is the biggest modern plague affecting our youth. The primary mission of the Holy Father is to shake us all out of our worldly complacency, but most especially our youth. Without them our future is lost. Hence his battle cry to young people: *Hagan lío!* "We didn't come into this world to 'vegetate', to take it easy, to make our lives a comfortable sofa to fall asleep on," he told hundreds of thousands of young people at the prayer vigil on the eve of World Youth Day in Poland in July 2016. "No, we came for another reason: to leave a mark. It is very sad to pass through life without leaving a mark."

On the lips of the Holy Father, *hagan lío!* is an order to shake off the anaesthesia, to leave the sofa behind, to get out of oneself to encounter others, especially the poor in our midst. When anaesthesia wears off, people become conscious and aware. Only then can we take the first step on the path to authentic relationships with others. Only then do we encounter Christ, who frees our hearts and minds from dependency on the anaesthesia. It is Christ who then becomes our hope and our strength to conquer the worldliness that surrounds us.

The Holy Father believes that if young people have an opportunity to know God they will gain strength and hope from him. In his encounter with young people in Paraguay in 2015, he told them: "That is what we need today, young people with hope, and young people with strength; we do not want young people who are weak, young people who simply are there, they are not a 'yes' and they are not a 'no,' we do not want young people who get tired easily or who live tired, with faces of boredom!" Pope Francis wants young people to be active and to be the primary agents of tenderness and mercy in the church and in the world.

On other occasions, the Holy Father has strongly opposed what he describes as the dominant "throwaway culture" where the elderly and the young are treated as disposable and excluded. He really does believe that our young people have the potential to transform the church into the "field hospital" he so desires. He believes in the youth of our parishes and communities; he is convinced they need to become protagonists in solving the ills that affect our world.

Young people are key to Pope Francis's efforts at revitalizing the church—sending it out and bringing it close to people. The vision of *Evangelii Gaudium* requires conversion. He wants the young to lead that change: to shake things up, to make holy *lío*, the type of *lío* that will suck out the anaesthesia from minds and hearts, freeing the church to be the primary source of mercy and compassion in our hurting world.

The pope has spoken, and he could not be clearer: *Hagan lío!*

Fr. Manuel Dorantes is pastor of Immaculate Conception Parish on 44th in Chicago, Illinois, serves as a strategic adviser to the Vatican's Secretariat for Communication, and tweets @TweetingPriest.

Hope

Natalia Imperatori-Lee

My youngest son, Benjamin, had a habit around the time he was three years old of asking impossible questions while we were all in the car. Both our sons, like all kids, are naturally curious, but Ben's questions have always been somewhat strange. "Mami, what is R?" "How do you use your neck?" "What's the smallest thing, including creatures?" These were regular parts of our family drives for a few years. We collected them into a list and named it "Zen with Ben." One of my favourite Zens with Ben is when he said, "Mami, do you want to think on the good side?"

To tell the truth, I have a lot of trouble doing that. I am an anxious pessimist, and I catastrophize, constantly thinking of worst-case scenarios. These days, it is easy to give in to hopelessness. In fact it is probably my frequent hopelessness that prompted my son's query. Pope Francis, however, offers us many lessons on the charism of hope. Ben's inscrutable question gets at the heart of what Pope Francis means (and doesn't mean) by "hope."

Pope Francis has a lot to say about hope. He has mentioned it in *Evangelii Gaudium* and *Amoris Laetitia*, he brings it up in interviews and addresses regularly, and he even devoted nearly eleven months of his weekly Wednesday audiences (from December 2016 to October 2017) to a catechism on hope. Throughout these documents and addresses, the pope makes clear that hope should be distinguished from optimism, that it is a gift particularly of the marginalized and suffering, and that hope is an expectation that entails solidarity and accompaniment.

The easiest way to approach Francis's notion of hope is to clarify, as he often does, what hope is *not*—it is not optimism, positive thinking, or thinking "on the good side" as my son would say. Optimism disappoints, said Francis in a Wednesday audience in December 2016. Because optimism relies on our human imagination and is founded on our achievements, it is antithetical to hope, which is based on the certainty of God's promises, confirmed in Jesus' resurrection. Similarly, in an interview with Fr. Antonio Spadaro, Pope Francis noted that optimism is a psychological disposition, whereas hope is a divine gift. To equate the two diminishes Christian hope to a human construct and limits God, reducing the divine to "fit our own template" (general audience, January 11, 2017). Hope, for Pope Francis, is first and foremost a gift that comes to us from God, and not a feeling, hunch, or outlook on life that is rooted primarily in human experience. Hope exceeds our expectations, resting on the certainty of God's promise, and this is why it sustains us in the Christian life.

A second characteristic of the pope's understanding of hope is its association with the "little ones," the poor and the marginalized. Francis frequently rails against the powerful who rest on their own certainties: "Those who are already full of themselves and of their achievements are not able to place their trust in anyone but themselves" and so are incapable of hope (general audience, February 1, 2017). Instead, for Pope Francis, hope is the prerogative of the poor, the marginalized and forgotten, and especially the suffering. Ironically, Francis spoke most eloquently about hope when he addressed prison chaplains in Italy in 2013. There, he noted that there is no cell so closed off that the hope of Christ cannot be present. On other occasions, he has said that tears produce hope, and that Christian hope entered the world at the incarnation, revealed to poor shepherds and other insignificant people. Hope teaches us that God aims to heal the wounded and humiliated. True hope, said Francis in May 2017, is never cheap; it always undergoes defeat. Suffering and hope go together as surely as self-satisfaction and disappointment.

A third and final characteristic of hope for Pope Francis is what I call "expectation plus." Hope is not optimism, but it is an expectation—Christian hope enables us to expect that God will deliver on the divine promises of salvation, consolation, and mercy. But this expectation is not an end in itself for us to passively enjoy while we wait for the end times. Rather, hope is expectation-plus-*solidarity* with those who suffer; it is expectation-plus-*accompaniment* in community; and it is expectation-plus-*journeying* in mission. For Francis, hope is born at the incarnation and revealed anew at the cross. In the incarnation, God becomes small, a child, a seed of new hope revealed to those who gather around the newborn Christ. But in the passion of the cross, Christ himself is split open like the seed that falls to the ground and germinates, and in Christ's death, our Christian hope is born. Thus Francis, at a Lenten Wednesday audience in April 2017, noted that "when we choose the hope of Jesus we find that the successful way of life is that of the seed . . . to give life, not keep it."

Hope impels us to embrace those who suffer. It demands, as Christ demanded of his followers, poverty and martyrdom. The expectation of Christian hope is the expectation of those in solidarity with the marginalized and humiliated, for only those who suffer know hope; those who rest on their earthly accomplishments have no need of it. But solidarity is not enough if it remains vague or merely volitional, shown only in thoughts and not in action. Pope Francis insists that hope shows forth in our accompaniment of those who suffer. As a gift of the Holy Spirit, said Francis in May 2016, hope enables us to be like the Paraclete, comforters who, through the Spirit's help, foster hope in all of creation. Drawing on the story of the disciples on the road to Emmaus, Pope Francis highlights that Jesus is able to restore their hope because he listens to the disciples, meets them where they are (defeated, on the road), and walks with them. Accompaniment is the key to hope, and also the key to community. The fostering of Christian hope is the responsibility of the whole church, for hope must be nourished. "If we hope," said the pope in February of 2017, "it is because many of our brothers and sisters have taught us to hope and have kept our hope alive." Thus, our hope must be fed in community, the community of the church that journeys together.

Finally, this accompaniment is not limited to the church community. Pope Francis frequently ties his reflections on hope to his ecclesiology. Hope is always journeying outward to the margins. He calls Lent a journey of hope. In an address to members of the Pontifical Council for Promoting the New Evangelization, he explicitly tied hope to the mission of the church: "The church is the home where doors are always open, not only because everyone finds a welcome and is able to breathe in love and hope, but also because we can go out bearing this love and hope." For Pope

Francis, hope is not oriented *ad intra*, towards the church as an end in itself or as a mechanism to sustain the church in hard times, though that is certainly a component of hope. Christian hope is an expectation that must journey outward, encountering the least of these and kindling hope in desperate situations like prisons, hospitals, and refugee camps. The church is a beacon of hope even as it is a respite for those who are hopeless, but it must also go outside its boundaries to encounter those who are in despair.

In the end, Benjamin's questioning is only in part a request for knowledge or a demand for answers and content. A three-year-old asks questions from the back seat of a car because he wants to know that someone is there, listening to him, that he is heard and valued and accompanied. Francis often speaks of children as symbols of hope, especially the smiles elicited when we encounter a child. Even if Christian hope cannot be reduced to "thinking on the good side," the outreach of a child's inquisitive mind, and the smile those memories still bring, are symbols of our certain hope in God's parental love, Christ's heroic sacrifice, and the Spirit's enlivening consolation.

Natalia Imperatori-Lee is associate professor of religious studies at Manhattan College in New York, teaching in the areas of ecclesiology, Latinx theology and gender studies. She is the author of Cuéntame: Narrative in the Ecclesial Present *(Orbis, 2018), and coeditor with Julia Brumbaugh of* Turning to the Heavens and the Earth: Theological Reflections on a Cosmological Conversion *(Liturgical Press, 2016). She lives in the Bronx with her spouse and two sons.*

Immigrant

Norma Seni Pimentel, MJ

I grew up in South Texas in the Rio Grande Valley, on the border between Mexico and the United States. I remember crossing as a child back and forth from Brownsville, Texas, to Matamoros, Tamaulipas, Mexico. We had family on both sides. We bought groceries on both sides. It was always better to purchase some things *en el otro lado* (on the other side) as we called the United States, but the best tortillas were from Matamoros. We saw each other as *hermanos*. It did not matter on which side of the border we were born. *Somos familia*; we are family.

Because we are all immigrants, our interconnected lives predispose those of us who have lived in the Rio Grande Valley to be people who are always ready to welcome other immigrants. We understand what it means to struggle and the need to help one another through the difficulties of life. When help is needed, people here on the border are always ready to help. While our area is counted among the poorest in the nation, our people are generous, giving what they can. When our border experienced an influx of immigrants from Central America in 2014, families brought food, clothing, and blankets and gave lovingly of their time. Together we welcomed the immigrant families in need of help. Everyone saw it as the right thing to do.

When Pope Francis addressed the US Congress in September 2015 he described himself as a "son of immigrants" and noted that, like me and my neighbours in the Rio Grande Valley, many of the senators and representatives could describe themselves the same way. With that connection established, Pope Francis told our legislators, "We, the people of this continent, are not fearful of foreigners, because most of us were once foreigners," and the task today is to "educate new generations not to turn their backs on our 'neighbours.'"

In the Americas, he said, "thousands of people are led to travel north in search of a better life for themselves and for their loved ones, in search of greater opportunities. Is this not what we want for our own children? We must not be taken aback by their numbers, but rather view them as people, seeing their faces and listening to their stories, trying to respond as best we can to their situation. To respond in a way which is always humane, just and fraternal."

I chuckle when I think of my own story of how I came to be a US citizen. My parents crossed into the United States one day to ask authorities what they needed to apply for residency. They were told that all they needed was to fill out an application. My father did so and was ready to go back to Mexico to wait for a response. To my parents' surprise, they were told they had to stay in the United States to await the response. My father found himself in a country where he knew no one and needed to find a place where his family (my mother and my oldest sister, Irasema) could stay. He had no money, no work, and no idea where to go. He found a place where he rented a room with the promise he would pay in a week. He then went to look for a job, which he found at a local food store sacking groceries. That was my family's beginning in the United States! At the time my mother was pregnant with me, and a few days later I was born. I am a US citizen by *chiripa*—sheer chance. I grew up *entre dos fronteras*, enjoying life in two countries, Mexico and the United States.

Migrants have always been a part of my life. At the convent, Sister Juliana Garcia—*que en paz descanse*—often received phone calls late at night from a border patrol officer. Each time the officer called, he would bring a Central American family in need of a place to stay for a couple of days. It was always a mother with her little child. Sometimes they were from El Salvador, Honduras, Guatemala, or Nicaragua. The stories of the many refugees we welcomed at the convent opened our understanding of the tragic reality of so many who are forced to flee their country due to the violence and the hardship of living in such danger.

Today we are experiencing a similar migration of refugees in our region; this time, however, they are mostly children. We see this crude human reality happening all over the world. People flee their home country because it is unsafe to remain there. Pope Francis has spoken in defence of the migrants and refugees to make sure that we do not remain indifferent to the suffering that we see. His voice is a reminder that we need to welcome and help them and that it is imperative to respond with care and compassion.

When Pope Francis recognized the work of so many volunteers at the Humanitarian Respite Center at Sacred Heart Church in McAllen, Texas, it felt as if God our Father, through the pope, was telling us: "You are my children; I love you very much. Continue to do my work in caring for my families who need help. Take care of them as I care for you."

Here in the Rio Grande Valley of South Texas, I experienced the full understanding of Pope Francis's message: his call to welcome the immigrants in our midst; his words of encouragement to be merciful; and his constant reminder to defend and protect the dignity of all humans, especially the frail, vulnerable, and those suffering from injustice in our world because of extreme poverty, violence, and war.

The encounter with the immigrant is a transforming experience that brings us face to face with God's mercy through their suffering. Walking into a bus station filled with immigrant families, mothers and infants in dire need of help, exhausted from their long journey through different countries, you can see in their eyes their immense pain and profound cry for help. As we lead them and walk them through the doors of our respite centre, they break into tears when welcomed by the many volunteers who express their love and compassion. The volunteers' smiles and friendly embraces serve as a healing salve. Hearing the stories of our immigrant brothers and sisters opens our hearts to hold them in a special place where we can accompany them in their suffering. We hear countless stories where time and time again immigrants endure extreme suffering and injustice caused by a selfish, corrupt, and sinful world; a world that has no respect for human dignity; a world that excuses indifference and exploitation of human life.

We need to ask ourselves: what is our response when we encounter an immigrant? Whether it is in our own community, our country, or in the news, Pope Francis invites us to respond with mercy and love. We cannot remain indifferent to human suffering. We must come together with courage and determination to transform our world into a kinder and more merciful place through a "revolution of tenderness," as Pope Francis inspires us to do through his own personal witness of humility and tenderness in all that he does and says. *Somos hermanos entre fronteras.*

Sr. Norma Pimentel is a member of the Missionaries of Jesus and executive director of Catholic Charities of the Rio Grande Valley in the Diocese of Brownsville, Texas.

Indifference

Carmen Sammut, MSOLA

In the book of Revelation, the faithful One says to the church in Laodicea: "I know your works; I know that you are neither cold nor hot. I wish you were either cold or hot " (3:15). Pope Francis seems to give us the same message by his frequent reference to our indifference, even to the "globalization of indifference." It is as if he wants to wake us up to our responsibility for our contemporaries, for the generations that will come after us, for our planet. He exhorted religious men and women during the year dedicated to consecrated life to "wake up the world," to live up to their mission. In *Evangelii Gaudium* he reminded us that we each are on "a mission on earth. . . . We have to regard ourselves as sealed, even branded, by this mission of bringing light, blessing, enlivening, raising up, healing and freeing" (273). The importance of each person for the well-being of the whole makes indifference even more deplorable.

During the pope's 2015 visit to the Philippines, a child asked him why so many children are abandoned by their parents and end up on the streets. She asked why God allowed something like this to happen, even to innocent children, and why there are so few who are helping them.

Francis had no answer to these questions and just allowed himself to ask: "Why do children suffer so much?" He asked the youth who were there to learn to weep when they see someone left on the side, someone who suffered abuse. And to learn to love and let oneself be loved (Santo Tomas University, January 18, 2015).

For alas, we often turn our faces away from the suffering of others: "When we are healthy and comfortable, we forget about others, we are unconcerned with their problems, their sufferings and the injustices they endure. . . . Our heart grows cold" (Message for Lent 2015).

Walking with a Vision

By calling us out of our indifference Pope Francis reveals to us something of his vision of God, of the person, of creation. God is the all-merciful Father, a God whose love is unlimited, to the point of giving us his Son for our salvation. "God is not indifferent to what happens to us. He knows us by name, cares for us and seeks us out whenever we turn away from him" (Message for Lent 2015). In this perspective, every person is of inestimable worth, a son or daughter of the Father. We all belong to the same family, brothers and sisters of each other. How could we be indifferent to what our brothers and sisters suffer? During the Eucharistic celebration marking the very start of his Petrine ministry, Francis asked all "to be protectors of God's gifts. . . . It means respecting each of God's creatures and respecting the environment in which we live" (Mass for inauguration of Petrine ministry, March 19, 2013).

In his message for the celebration of the 44th World Day of Peace on January 1, 2016, "Overcome indifference and win peace," Francis explained that our society is often indifferent to God and we "think that we are the source and creator of ourselves, our lives and society." This in turn "leads to indifference to one's neighbour and to the environment." We might be aware of the tragedies, but we do nothing to help those suffering; or we turn our head and blame others for their misfortunes. We do not care about the state of health of our common home. All this "prolongs situations of injustice and grave social imbalance, which in turn lead to conflict." In his 2015 encyclical letter on the environment, *Laudato Si'*, he asks us "what kind of world do we want to leave to those who come after us, to children who are growing up?" (160). He calls us to examine the deep purpose of our life and to care for our common home as well as for our brothers and sisters who live in it. One cannot go without the other.

Leading by Example

Pope Francis does not only preach against indifference. It seems that every suffering in the world, in people and in creation, affects him personally. He does not only send out messages of hope, he goes out to bring the message himself, to be the message. This came across very strongly as he walked, alone, in the concentration camp of Auschwitz-Birkenau in July 2016 in deep silence as if carrying on his shoulders the pain of those who were killed, the horror lived there, the sinfulness of our humanity. "Lord, have mercy on your people! Lord, forgiveness for so much cruelty!" he wrote in the camp's guestbook.

His first trip as pope in July 2013 was to Lampedusa, the little island off the shores of Italy where so many migrants have died while seeking better lives. It is also an island where so many migrants have been rescued and welcomed. Another trip took Francis to the Greek island of Lesbos in April 2016, where he said he "saw the sorrow of war in the eyes of the refugees, the anguish of peoples thirsting for peace." He brought with him back to Rome three refugee families from Syria—twelve people in all, including six children—hoping that other states would follow his example and become more willing to welcome refugees.

His example carries and, as he explained in his January 2016 peace message, many—individuals, families, non-governmental and charitable organizations, journalists and photographers, defenders of human rights, young people—are striving to join forces in an effort to globalize compassion and create a culture of encounter and of solidarity.

A Call to Structural Change

Pope Francis's great wish is to see a change of heart as well as of structures. He knows that for change to last it needs a transformation of the mind and the heart as well as of societal and church structures. He calls us to prayer, for "together with the saints . . . we form part of that communion in which indifference is conquered by love" (Message for Lent 2015). This ensures that we drop "our pretentions to self-sufficiency." Secondly, he calls us to be engaged especially with those on the peripheries of society.

He calls for structural changes and asks national leaders for better conditions for prisoners, for the sick, for migrants, for concrete gestures in favour of those deprived of labour, land, and lodging. He calls leaders to cooperate concretely in order to work for peace beyond their borders. He often specifically asks that women be given their rightful place, within the church and society, so that they can give their full share in the building of our common home.

We know that all changes of mentality and of structures take much time and effort. We hope that more and more of us, within and outside the church, will answer Pope Francis's call to have eyes and see, have ears and hear, to let our hearts be converted and our arms and feet drawn towards the other. Let us strive to build a culture of compassion.

Sr. Carmen Sammut is the superior general of the Missionary Sisters of Our Lady of Africa. She is also the president of the International Union of Superiors General, the Rome-based umbrella organization of global women religious, and previously spent twenty-eight years as a teacher in Algeria, Tunisia, and Mauritania.

Jesus

Agbonkhianmeghe E. Orobator, SJ

Versatility characterizes Pope Francis's use of "Jesus." Jesus is a name, not just any other word. Jesus is the sum of Christian proclamation of salvation.

A vital key to understanding Francis's use of the name "Jesus" is his motto, *Miserando atque Eligendo* ("By Having Mercy and by Choosing Him"). Francis borrowed the phrase from the homilies of Bede the Venerable, who made a poignant comment on the gospel story of the calling of Matthew: Jesus looked upon Matthew with merciful love and chose him. Jesus' look was so full of mercy it forgave Matthew's sins. In a 2013 interview with Jesuit Fr. Antonio Spadaro, Francis would later add: "That finger of Jesus, pointing at Matthew. That's me. I feel like him. Like Matthew." Jesus as that look full of mercy serves a revelatory purpose: "Jesus Christ is the face of the Father's mercy" (*Misericordiae Vultus* 1).

Jesus as face or the face of Jesus is a recurring theme for Francis. There are variant and simultaneous renditions—face, look, and gaze. As face, Jesus is beautiful and merciful; as look, Jesus overflows with mercy and compassion; and as gaze, Jesus is forgiving and loving (homily, May 17, 2013). Jesus' look elicits multiple reactions and registers varied impacts. His look stirs amazement, invites discipleship, and causes joy (homily, July 5, 2013). For Francis, as merciful face, Jesus is anything but a dry-cleaner in the confessional (homily, April 29, 2013). "A concrete sign of the constancy of divine love that pardons and saves," Jesus is mercy incarnate—patient and gazing, forgiving and loving, transforming and summoning (MV 17). Jesus' words are like music spoken by a shepherd to the sheep.

Besides face, Jesus is a synonym for many things. Some familiar, like hope. But others not: like a trouble-maker "who creates so many problems" (homily, September 26, 2013). Jesus is a "door" leading out of our exodus towards the Father, the wounds of Jesus, and the wounds of others (homily, May 11, 2013). Jesus is the true door; we knock at and pass through this door to access the Father's love, mercy, and life (homily, April 22, 2013). Jesus is priest and intercessor (homily, May 11, 2013).

Francis's rich Jesus vocabulary and symbols do not reify Jesus, either as idea or abstraction. Jesus is a person, the subject of a personal encounter in the circumstances of daily living. "We only come to know Jesus on the daily path of life" (homily, September 26, 2013). Jesus meets us where we are (homily, May 18, 2013). "I invite all Christians, everywhere, at this very moment, to a renewed personal encounter with Jesus Christ, or at least an openness to letting him encounter them" (*Evangelii Gaudium* 3). Jesus is someone who not only challenges us, but who we can challenge in prayer (homily, May 3, 2013). "Ask Jesus what he wants from you and be brave!" Jesus speaks to the heart to initiate conversion. Thus knowing Jesus requires "heart knowledge" and meeting Jesus occasions faith and brings joy and peace (homily, May 16, 2013).

Yet the encounter with Jesus can bother and unsettle us. Jesus healed, taught, and upbraided people. But Jesus is more than just a healer, teacher, and revolutionary. Jesus is a reconciler of people to God in his own flesh. Jesus is a builder of bridges, not walls. Jesus is present and works in the church in the power of the Holy Spirit.

Francis sees a radical concreteness about Jesus' salvific mission: "Jesus didn't save us by an idea or intellectual programme. He saved us with his flesh, with his own actual flesh" (homily, June 14, 2013). In Jesus the incarnation is real: "I believe in Jesus Christ, his incarnation" (interview with *La Repubblica*, October 1, 2013).

Strikingly, Jesus is a potent antidote for modern-day vices flagged by Francis as "temptations" in the church. Vices such as careerism, gossiping or interfering with people's lives and tearing each other apart, triumphalism, slander, and hypocrisy. Appropriately, Jesus is the one who offers an alternative way. The way of Jesus is synonymous with the cross, which in human terms "ended in failure" (homily, September 24, 2015).

This way of the cross takes patience, nurtured by silence and peace. To be a Christian is to walk along the way of Jesus, the way of the cross and persecution. Jesus is the wounded one, whose wound is visible in the flesh of the hungry, thirsty, naked, humiliated, prisoners, and the sick. In them we touch, stroke, cure, and kiss the wounds and flesh of Jesus.

Jesus doesn't fit into our familiar staid logic. Jesus does things his own way and when he thinks it's best (homilies, June 28 and July 25, 2013). Francis doesn't shy from putting words in Jesus' mouth to drive home a point: "Jesus says quite simply, 'Don't speak ill of anyone, don't belittle them, don't discredit them. Basically we are walking along the same road'" (homily, June 13, 2013); "Jesus tells us, 'Don't be afraid! Fear doesn't help us'" (homily, July 2, 2013); "Jesus tells us what the 'protocol' is on which we will be judged. It is the one we read in chapter 25 of Matthew's Gospel" (*This Economy Kills*, Liturgical Press, 2015).

In Francis's lexicon, "Jesus" is real, personal, challenging, comforting, disturbing, renewing. His Jesus quotes would make for a prayerful litany, as the following sample suggests.

Jesus is:

- "my teacher and my pastor."
- "the rock that gives us freedom."
- "God's mercy."
- "always beside us."
- "prayer."

Jesus:

- "never lets you down."
- "causes amazement."
- "opens the door of the house to us."
- "looks at someone with mercy, changes their life and has a party."

Fr. Agbonkhianmeghe E. Orobator is a Jesuit priest and president of the Conference of Major Superiors of Africa and Madagascar.

Joy

Timothy Radcliffe, OP

The face of Pope Francis, the best known in the world, is nearly always filled with joy and so it is fitting that his first apostolic exhortation should be called "The Joy of the Gospel." " 'The identity card of a Christian is his joy, the joy of the Gospel, the joy of having been chosen by Jesus, saved by Jesus, regenerated by Jesus; the joy of the hope that Jesus is waiting for us. . . . In the crosses and sufferings of this life,' Christians live that joy, expressing it in another way, with the 'peace' that comes from the 'assurance that Jesus accompanies us, that he is with us'" (homily, May 23, 2016). We cannot preach the Gospel if we are "sourpusses" (*Evangelii Gaudium* 85).

This joy that pervades all that Pope Francis says and does is not just an emotion or a forced jollity. It is a sharing in the very being of God, the mutual delight of the Trinity. The promise of the Lord is that "I will give you a new heart, and a new spirit I will put within you. I will remove the heart of stone from your flesh and give you a heart of flesh" (Ezek 36:26). A heart of flesh will feel both pain and joy. The contrary of joy is a dead heart unable to feel anything at all. Indeed, suffering can hollow a space for a larger joy than we could have imagined.

In *Amoris Laetitia*, Francis assures us that the joy of a marriage may be deepened by shared trial: "Joy also grows through pain and sorrow. In the words of Saint Augustine, 'the greater the danger in battle the greater is the joy of victory.' After suffering and struggling together, spouses are able to experience that it was worth it, because they achieved some good, learned something as a couple, or came to appreciate what they have. Few human joys are as deep and thrilling as those experienced by two people who love one another and have achieved something as the result of a great, shared effort" (130).

Francis's first expedition from Rome after his election was to Lampedusa, the island near which so many refugees fleeing Africa have perished. He lamented that we had lost our capacity to be touched by their pain, which means also a shrinking of our capacity for joy. In Buenos Aires as archbishop he was not so constantly joyful, pained by the suffering of his people. All this gave him a heart of flesh that overflows with the joy he now shares with the world.

This joy is to be shared with everyone, as boundless as the universe. "The joy of the Gospel is for all people: no one can be excluded. That is what the angel proclaimed to the shepherds in Bethlehem: 'Be not afraid; for behold, I bring you good news of a great joy which will come to all the people' (Lk 2:10). The Book of Revelation speaks of 'an eternal Gospel to proclaim to those who dwell on earth, to every nation and tongue and tribe and people' (Rev 14:6)" (EG 23).

At Jesus' baptism, the voice of the father is heard: "You are my beloved Son; with you I am well pleased" (Mark 1:11). This delight overflows into Jesus' celebration of people whose secret goodness is disclosed to him. We are called to be bearers of God's own joy especially in the despised and rejected.

This joy comes to expression in the human face, first of all that of Jesus but also our own. Francis's own joy springs from his conviction that the Lord has smiled on him. "I am one who is looked upon by the Lord," Francis said in a 2013 interview with Jesuit Fr. Antonio Spadaro—like the rich man whom the Lord looked upon with love, like the Caravaggio of Matthew: "Here, this is me, a sinner on whom the Lord has turned his gaze." The good news was incarnated in the penetrating and tender gaze of Jesus. He saw little Zacchaeus hidden in his tree, and the widow putting her money in the temple treasury. That gaze rests on us. "Standing before him with open hearts, letting him look at us, we see that gaze of love which Nathaniel glimpsed on the day when Jesus said to him: 'I saw you under the fig tree' (Jn 1:48)" (EG 264).

The delight of the Lord in us draws us out of self-preoccupation, liberating us from the sad introversion that suffocates all pleasure in life and love. "Thanks solely to this encounter—or renewed encounter—with God's love, which blossoms into an enriching friendship, we are liberated from our narrowness and self-absorption. We become fully human when we become more than human, when we let God bring us beyond ourselves in order to attain the fullest truth of our being" (EG 8).

This liberation from self-centredness engages with two other themes of Francis's understanding of joy. First of all, our greatest joy is in the joy of others. The more we delight in their happiness, the deeper shall be our own. "Our Lord especially appreciates those who find joy in the happiness of others. If we fail to learn how to rejoice in the well-being of others, and focus primarily on our own needs, we condemn ourselves to a joyless existence, for, as Jesus said, 'it is more blessed to give than to receive' (Acts 20:35)" (*Amoris Laetitia* 110). The family should be the school of such altruistic joy.

Secondly, true happiness flourishes when we are freed from enslavement to possessions. Think of the rich man who rejected Jesus' invitation to leave everything and follow him: "He was shackled to his belongings! Jesus told us that one cannot serve two masters: either one must serve God or serve riches. Riches are not bad in themselves, but slavery to wealth—this, is wickedness. The poor young man went away sad . . . 'He frowned and he went away sorrowful'" (homily, May 23, 2016).

Francis's critique of the dreary consumerist mentality comes to fullest expression so far in *Laudato Si'*, a delight in the whole of creation which joyfully sings God's praise by its very existence. This dissolves the desire to devour the world and see it solely as for our exploitation. "We need to take up an ancient lesson, found in different religious traditions and also in the Bible. It is the conviction that 'less is more.' A constant flood of new consumer goods can baffle the heart and prevent us from cherishing each thing and each moment" (222). He quotes the bishops of Japan: "To sense each creature singing the hymn of its existence is to live joyfully in God's love and hope" (85). May it ignite our hearts too!

Fr. Timothy Radcliffe is a former Master of the Order of Preachers and an itinerant preacher and teacher.

Judgment

Michael J. O'Loughlin

For good or ill, a single sound bite sometimes sums up the essence of an entire papacy. Take Pope Leo X. A scion of the storied Medici family and a patron of the arts, Leo had a penchant for luxury. Upon his election, he purportedly uttered, "Since God has given us the papacy, let us enjoy it." And he did enjoy it, draining the Vatican treasury to fund lavish renovations and massive art projects, including the completion of St. Peter's Basilica. (To bring in more revenue, he expanded the sale of indulgences, leading to the Protestant Reformation. Oops.)

There are plenty of more recent, if less dramatic, examples of sound bites cutting through the noise to get at the heart of a papacy.

When asked why he was convening the Second Vatican Council, Pope John XXIII is reported to have said, "I want to throw open the windows of the church so that we can see out and the people can see in." He was responsible for some of the biggest changes in church history, which elevated the role of the laity and prodded church leaders towards transparency.

Then, with the world on the brink of nuclear annihilation in the 1960s, Pope Paul VI proclaimed to the United Nations, "Never again war, never again war!" John Paul II, understanding the anxiety gripping the planet as the Cold War continued, began his papacy with, "Be not afraid!" Sensing a change to the challenges facing the church by the mid-2000s, Pope Benedict XVI warned in a speech delivered just before his election, "We are building a dictatorship of relativism."

Those sound bites help us understand the priorities and personalities of the popes, and while it's perhaps too early to speculate which sound bite will ultimately define Pope Francis, at this point in his papacy, it's hard to imagine anything coming close to a question he asked in 2013: "Who am I to judge?"

The context of that remark, which was seemingly reported by every Catholic and secular news outlet, is important.

It came just four months after his election, when the world was still not quite sure what to make of the first pope to hail from the Americas. Francis was on a plane, heading back to Rome from World Youth Day in Rio de Janeiro. At the start of the trip, he told journalists that he does not give many interviews because he is uncomfortable trying to communicate in that fashion. But on the flight home, he agreed to hold a press conference, the start of a tradition that would create some of the biggest and boldest headlines during his papacy.

An Italian journalist asked him a question about gay priests working in the Vatican, specifically wondering if there is a "gay lobby" with undue influence in the church. Francis said there was no evidence of a gay lobby, and he then pivoted to talk about gay people more generally.

"If a person is gay and seeks the Lord and has good will, well who am I to judge them?" the pope asked.

It was a simple question that nonetheless would go on to define the papacy of a pastor whom the world was just getting to know.

The pope's question held obvious appeal for LGBT Catholics and their families. For one thing, Francis actually used the word gay—a first for a pope. (Many Catholic leaders employ the more clinical sounding phrase "same-sex attraction" when talking about gays and lesbians, often over the objection of the people they are talking about.) It also signalled an openness from the highest echelons of the church towards accompanying gays and lesbians on their faith journeys, something relatively novel in recent church history.

In the weeks and months that followed, some Catholic pundits, concerned that the church's emphasis on the sinfulness of homosexual sex was being lost amid the more welcome tone of the pope, tried to walk back the comment. They pointed out that Pope Francis is against same-sex marriage, that he is troubled by what he calls "gender ideology," which posits that gender is a social construct, and that he has not changed any church teaching on sexual morality. That is all true.

But when Pope Francis had the opportunity in 2016 to address the comment himself, he repeated his assertion that gays and lesbians should not be marginalized in the church.

"On that occasion I said this: If a person is gay and seeks out the Lord and is willing, who am I to judge that person?" Francis told the Italian journalist Andrea Tornelli in a book-length interview called *The Name of God is Mercy*. "I was paraphrasing by heart the Catechism of the Catholic Church where it says that these people should be treated with delicacy and not be marginalized."

"I am glad that we are talking about 'homosexual people' because before all else comes the individual person, in his wholeness and dignity," he continues. "And people should not be defined only by their sexual tendencies: let us not forget that God loves all his creatures and we are destined to receive his infinite love."

As for how gay and lesbian Catholics should practise the faith? No different from anyone else, the pope suggested.

"I prefer that homosexuals come to confession, that they stay close to the Lord, and that we pray all together," he said. "You can advise them to pray, show goodwill, show them the way, and accompany them along it."

Of course, the pope's comments and his desire to rid the church of excessive judgment extend far beyond his thoughts about the LGBT community. In fact, resisting judgmentalism pops up again and again in the pope's writings, homilies, and addresses.

In *Evangelii Gaudium*, or "The Joy of the Gospel," which Pope Francis published during the first year of his pontificate and which serves as the blueprint of his papacy, he wrote what has become another of his famous lines. He said that he prefers a church that is "bruised, hurting and dirty because it has been out on the streets, rather than a church which is unhealthy from being confined and from clinging to its own security." One of the symptoms of the church being closed in on itself, he continued, is that it makes Christians fixate on "rules which make us harsh judges."

A little later in the document, Francis writes about the traits for effective evangelization, which he said includes "certain attitudes which foster openness to the message: approachability, readiness for dialogue, patience, a warmth and *welcome which is non-judgmental*" (emphasis added).

Why the focus on judgment? Sure, in the gospels, Jesus repeatedly warns his followers against judging others. So Pope Francis is certainly drawing on good source material. But he's actually trying to make a broader point.

He may go down in history as the "Who am I to judge?" pope, but the question he asks points to a Christian virtue much more important to Francis: *mercy*. To put it succinctly, Pope Francis believes that the world has forgotten what it means to be merciful and that being overly judgmental prevents us from showing mercy to others.

He laid out this argument in a homily delivered at his residence in 2014, as reported by *L'Osservatore Romano*. He said that being merciful includes seeking forgiveness for one's own sins—rather than condemning the shortcomings of others. "Who am I to judge this? Who am I to gossip about this? Who I am, who have done the same things, or worse?" he asked.

By adopting an attitude free of judging others, the pope argues, the world will be a more peaceful place.

"If all of us, all peoples, all families, all quarters had this attitude, how much peace there would be in the world, how much peace there would be in our hearts, for mercy brings us peace!" he said. "Let us always remember: Who am I to judge?"

Michael J. O'Loughlin is the national correspondent for America *and the author of* The Tweetable Pope: A Spiritual Revolution in 140 Characters.

Justice

Simone Campbell, SSS

At first glance, Pope Francis's sense of justice sounds a bit far removed from the gritty reality of the twenty-first century. In his exhortation *Evangelii Gaudium* he notes that living in dignity and right relationship can only happen when there is a true pursuit of the common good. He says: "Growth in justice requires more than economic growth, while presupposing such growth; it requires decisions, programmes, mechanisms and processes specifically geared to a better distribution of income, the creation of sources of employment and an integral promotion of the poor which goes beyond a simple welfare mentality" (EG 204). This sounds a little philosophical and ethereal.

But as I reflected on his words, I realized that for Pope Francis justice is visceral. He notes that for those in power it is "irksome when the question of ethics is raised, when global solidarity is invoked, when the distribution of goods is mentioned" (EG 203). I have experienced this. One time when lobbying now-US House Speaker Paul Ryan, I shared the concern about a family I met in Milwaukee who relied on food stamps to feed themselves and their two boys. Both parents were working, but they needed food stamps to get by. Congressman Ryan was proposing to cut food stamps for families like this one. When I raised this with him, in frustration he blurted out "but they are not the targets of my programme." I quietly added that they were going to be its victims, and that was wrong.

But rather than focus on those who have power and are disgruntled, Pope Francis embraces the anguish of those who have been left out. It is this anguish expressed in *Laudato Si'* that challenges us: "Today, however, we have to realize that a true ecological approach *always* becomes a social approach; it must integrate questions of justice in debates on the environment, so as to hear *both the cry of the earth and the cry of the poor*" (LS 49).

It is this cry that is at the heart of Pope Francis's quest for justice.

This insight heightened my awareness to the cries all around me so that we as a people might take steps towards justice. Most recently I have been in the midst of a struggle about access to healthcare in our nation. Where is justice in the midst of this political struggle? During my travels with NETWORK's Nuns on the Bus, I came to realize that politicians often seal themselves off from the literal cry of their constituents in order to further their partisan agenda. This ensures that justice will not be done. But to achieve justice we must open ourselves to the literal cry of those around us.

Joe McGrath called us at NETWORK Lobby for Catholic Social Justice in tears because he was so worried about his daughter Maura, who has Down's syndrome. She is just turning eighteen and will be dependent upon Medicaid for her survival. Joe is so worried that with Republican efforts to cut Medicaid she will be left out and left behind. He knows that his family does not have the resources to care for Maura and ensure that she lives in dignity. Who are we as a nation that we would cut Maura off from care? Joe's cry stirs my heart for justice.

Maria at St. Elizabeth's Center in Tucson, Arizona, weeps in fear that she will lose her Medicaid coverage. In 2009, she lost her job and her health insurance in the recession and went without care. When the Affordable Care Act took effect in Arizona she was able to get on Medicaid in 2013. When she saw a physician for the first time in four years, she was referred to a gynaecologist. In the course of a hysterectomy, it was discovered that she had second stage ovarian cancer. She has now had four recurrences, three surgeries, and chemotherapy. She worries about what will happen if she loses her healthcare again. She wants to continue to support her children and grandchildren. Maria brings tears to my eyes in her concern for herself and her family.

Joe and Maria's tears break my heart and change my perspective. This is at the heart of the quest for justice. Their tears lead me to state unequivocally that it is morally wrong to leave our people without access to healthcare. Healthcare is a right, not a privilege for the rich.

Perhaps what is most important is Pope Francis's knowledge that justice is not in the clouds, but is anchored in the stories of Joe and Maria.

Knowing their stories fuels my passion that all can live in dignity—this is justice. Once my heart has been broken open, then I can't stop on the journey to justice. It is urgent for the healing of our nation. But there is an additional truth.

My heart was broken open by the story of Margaret who lost her healthcare in the recession and then lost her life in 2012 before the full implementation of the Affordable Care Act. In June of 2012 I received Margaret's picture from her sister Jini and her partner Lynne. I carry that picture with me, and Margaret has fuelled my passion for justice in healthcare. But an additional piece of the story is that in 2014, in Lexington, Kentucky, a woman came up to me and said that she was one of Margaret's sisters. She told me that she wanted to thank me for helping to heal their family! It turns out that my speaking about Margaret's death helped the family make sense of an otherwise senseless death. I was nourishment to them just as Margaret was nourishment to me.

This is the deeper truth. When our hearts are broken open and we respond in the open-hearted quest for justice and the common good, then there is healing and community in many ripple effects. This is the Gospel justice that Pope Francis speaks of. Woven together in stories of heartbreak and hope, we become the beloved community that has justice at its core. Stirred by the cries around us, we speak up for the common good. We are called to react in love, share our resources, and forgive our failing. In short, we strive to establish justice in our midst.

Justice then is not an ethereal philosophical thought. Pope Francis's justice is rooted in the ground of people's lives and watered with their tears. When we weep together, we cannot be silent in the face of policies that shred human dignity. When we weep together, we will move towards justice.

Let this be our political action for justice in our economy and society. Let us respond to the cries around us. Let our hearts be broken open. Then we shall have justice flowing like water and integrity like an unfailing stream (Amos 5:24). This is Pope Francis's view of justice in these challenging times.

Sr. Simone Campbell is executive director of NETWORK Lobby for Catholic Social Justice and leader of the "Nuns on the Bus" campaign. She is a member of the Sisters of Social Service, an attorney, and a poet based in Washington, DC.

Leadership

Kerry Alys Robinson

"If you like Pope Francis, you're going to love Jesus Christ," quips a close friend and Jesuit priest. It's funny, but true.

For the most prominent, widely admired person on the global stage today leadership is entirely about serving others, and doing so with humility and mercy. "The world tells us to seek success, power and money; God tells us to seek humility, service and love," offers Pope Francis. "To change the world we must be good to those who cannot repay us." And in his surprise TED talk he entreated his worldwide audience to "Please, allow me to say it loud and clear: the more powerful you are, the more your actions will have an impact on people, the more responsible you are to act humbly. . . . Through humility and concrete love power becomes a service, a force for good."

When it comes to leadership, Francis emulates what he advocates. His hallmarks for effective, meaningful leadership include a profound commitment to mission, empathic mercy, joy, dialogue, vision, accountability, and to communicate and inspire these attributes in others. The pope's authenticity stems from his radical belief in God and commitment to be Christlike. He says what he means and his actions match his words, with uncommon consistency. As the successor of St. Peter, he is, in his own words, "not a star, but the servant of the servants of God." The greater the leader, the further out extends the leader's vision. Pope Francis has his eye on the eternal horizon and future generations not yet born. He trusts in providence. He relies on grace and prayer, especially ours, requesting our prayers at each and every encounter.

He exudes empathy. He spends his time in refugee camps, in hospitals, in prisons, in countries torn apart by war. He celebrated his birthday with eight homeless women and men. He routinely calls the mobile phones of people who have suffered to offer encouragement and prayer. He speaks truth to power and reminds us of who we are called to be at our best: sisters and brothers in a human family of more than seven billion. His leadership is entirely oriented to the welfare of others and he enjoins all Christians and people of good will to be likewise disposed. He brings good news, forgiveness, hope and God's love to all he encounters, seeking out those most in need.

Positive managerial reform is, emphatically, a signature of his pontificate. During the first year after his election he established the Secretariat for the Economy within the Holy See to promote accountability and the proper care of human and financial resources within the Vatican. He makes it clear that he expects financial accountability and desires "a poor church for the poor." A modern-day prophet, he reads the signs of the times and awakens us to meaningful change in our behaviour—within the church and within the world—evoking fear and joyful expectation in equal measure. Complex global challenges like forced migration, extreme poverty, human trafficking and climate change do not intimidate him; they only break his heart and command responsive action. He sees the church as "a field hospital," insists that his pastors have "the smell of the sheep," urges us to reach out to the margins, find our common humanity, and understand how encapsulating is God's love and tenderness. He prioritizes ecumenical and interfaith dialogue for the sake of the world and of God. At eighty-one he is a master communicator, the first truly "tweetable pope," whose injunctions in 140 characters or less, in multiple languages, are consistently uplifting and ennobling.

Powerful images of Pope Francis pull at the heart and stir the imagination: iconic images of him washing and kissing the feet of inmates, of women, of Muslims; exuberant selfies with teenagers; joyful interactions with newly married couples and children; and his loving, tactile embrace of a fifty-three-year-old man afflicted with neurofibromatosis.

He admonishes clergy who are sourpusses and insists that the joy of the Gospel be promulgated by our very lives. He asks every Catholic parish in Europe to welcome a refugee family and sets the example by sponsoring two families in Vatican apartments. He goes to confession. He buses his own tray. He bows his head and asks for our blessing before giving his inaugural blessing as pope. He declines the apostolic palace in favour of a simple room at Santa Marta, preferring to live in community for the health of his psyche and his soul.

In his first interview—at a time when the entire world's attention was on him—he was asked to define who Jorge Mario Bergoglio is. The newly elected pope replied without hesitation, "I am a sinner." And with that, he rendered himself immediately relatable to all of us. It was in a subsequent press conference, however, on a plane filled with journalists, that his most memorable sentence was offered. Only five words, it is a response to a question about homosexual people. Stressing the wholeness and dignity of each individual person destined to receive God's love, he answered, "Who am I to judge?" He insists on dialogue and seeks out diverse viewpoints. "As religious leaders, we are called to be true 'people of dialogue,' to cooperate in building peace not as intermediaries but as authentic mediators," he insists. "Each one of us is called to be an artisan of peace, by uniting and not dividing, by extinguishing hatred and not holding on to it, by opening paths to dialogue and not by constructing new walls!"

But of all the images of Pope Francis, there is one that is crucial to understanding the strength of his leadership, although we know about it only through his description. Shortly after his election, before he greets the crowd gathered in St Peter's Square, he is entreated by his friend and brother cardinal, Cardinal Claudio Hummes: "Don't forget the poor." He chooses the name Francis. The enormity of the responsibility that has been placed upon him cannot be exaggerated. The resistance he will experience cannot be overstated. He will soon set out to raise our consciousness to the stark realities of the materially poor, refugees, victims of violence and war, and the precarious environmental health of our common home. The sexual abuse crisis, the role of women in the church, modern understandings of human sexuality, and political divisiveness within the church and world will persistently demand his attention. Against this tableau, imagine this: Pope Francis bowing his head in prayer, emptying himself of all that stands between God and him. It is evocative of Christ in the Garden of Gethsemane, a complete surrendering to God's intent, with perfect trust. An enormous freedom, especially from fear, is conferred on him. He accedes to global leadership he neither desired nor sought.

We are drawn to his leadership. He restores our faith in humankind. He ennobles us. He calls us to be the very best people we can be, are intended to be. He inspires us to love more deeply, to encounter and accompany others, to be merciful, and to be faithful. He eschews fame, power, wealth, attention. He points us to Christ as if to say, "Don't follow me. Follow Him."

Kerry Alys Robinson is the founding executive director and global ambassador of Leadership Roundtable.

Legalism

Teresa Forcades i Vila, OSB

> Jesus, through his preaching and the total gift of himself that would lead him to the Cross, returned the Mosaic Law to its true and original intent. Here what is central is not the law or legal justice, but the love of God, which is capable of looking into the heart of each person and seeing the deepest desire hidden there; God's love must take primacy over all else.
> —*Misericordia et misera* 1

L

"What is central is not the law or legal justice, but the love of God." This is the basic preaching of Jesus, the central nerve of the Good News anticipated by the biblical prophets and sharpened by St. Paul: "for the letter brings death, but the Spirit gives life" (2 Cor 3:6). The term "legalism" as such appears rarely in Pope Francis's public speeches, but he speaks very often against "doctors of the law" that build closed systems of norms and justifications in order to appease their existential insecurity and then relentlessly impose them on others in the name of God. This is a frequent theme of the pope's daily homilies at Casa Santa Marta. In a January 2015 homily, Francis said such doctors of the law claim to be secure in their teaching "but as a man or woman in a prison cell is secure behind the bars: it's a security without freedom." In an October 2016 homily, the pope said those who place the law at the centre of their lives are prisoners, hypocrites, or sick. Francis cites freely Matthew 23:15, saying in a May 2016 homily: "For you travel half the world to make a single proselyte and then you turn him into a slave."

Against the aridity and narrow-mindedness of legalism, Francis proclaims: "You are just because God has come close to you, because God caresses you, because God tells you beautiful things with tenderness" (homily, December 11, 2014).

What a radical shift that is! "Being just" not because of "doing the right thing" but because of being thoroughly and gratuitously loved, like a child in its mother's lap—and because of being forgiven. To most of Jesus' religious contemporaries, this sounded outrageous, an undermining of religion itself, a blasphemy (homily, October 13, 2014). To Jesus (and to Francis) it is no blasphemy and no undermining of religion but its fulfilment: "returning the Mosaic Law to its true and original intent"—that is, realizing that we live by grace, out of love. We human beings are truly free because we came into existence through love and are kept alive by love; we are not the result of any blind mechanism, any chain of cause and effect, any system or any law.

In his January 1, 2015, Angelus meditation, Francis paraphrased Mark's Gospel, saying the Sabbath (or the law) was made for us and not we for the Sabbath. During that meditation, Francis also commented at length on Paul's letter to the Galatians. "Christ has taken up the human condition, freeing it from the closed, legalistic mentality," said the pope. "In fact, the law deprived of grace becomes an insupportable yoke, and instead of being good for us it is bad for us. . . . The redemption occurred with the death of Jesus Christ in the Cross. . . . Incorporated in Him, men and women really become children of God."

The law is not an end in itself, as legalism would have it. The goal of the law is to enable our return to God, like the prodigal son, so that we might receive adoption (Gal 4:5). We don't need adoption because we can cease to be God's children in God's eyes (to grasp the unconditionality and the depth of God's love for us, Francis recommends meditating on Isaiah 41:13-20), but because we can be won over by fear and mistrust and allow God to stop being the beloved Father-Mother in our eyes. Like in the Garden of Eden, we then hide from God, from each other and even from ourselves (Gen 3:7-10). As Francis said in his December 11, 2014, homily: "If we had the courage to open our heart to this tenderness of God, how much spiritual freedom we would have! How much!"

The legalistic mentality is unable to experience grace; it perceives it as a threat, a danger, a subversion. And indeed it is! Grace subverts all and any system that tries to objectify the human experience and rob it of its uniqueness. Each human is unique and must be regarded as such under all circumstances, no matter how deep or vicious his or her crime: *the love of God is capable of looking into the heart of each person and seeing the deepest desire hidden there.* That is why the law, precious as it is, will always be insufficient and that is why "we have to walk with these two things that Jesus teaches us: truth and understanding" (homily, May 29, 2016).

Besides the fundamental objectivity of the truth, we need an equally fundamental attention to subjectivity, to particularity. In his apostolic exhortation *Amoris Laetitia*, Francis stated: "It is reductive simply to consider whether or not an individual's actions correspond to a general law or rule, because that is not enough to discern and ensure fidelity to God in the concrete life of a human being" (AL 304). After that phrase in the exhortation, the pope cited St. Thomas Aquinas's *Summa Theologiae*: "Although there is necessity in the general principles, the more we descend to matters of detail, the more frequently we encounter defects. . . . In matters of action, truth or practical rectitude is not the same for all, as to matters of detail, but only as to the general principles."

We need to discern in each particular case and we need, above all, to acknowledge that there is only one Judge, who is in heaven and that "we are all sinners on the road" towards that Truth which is God's self (homily, May 20, 2016). As Francis said in his October 6, 2016, homily: "Attachment to the law ignores the Holy Spirit" and does not allow "that the power of Christ's redemption proceeds by means of the Spirit." On the contrary, "when a person is open to the Holy Spirit, he or she is like a sailboat swept by the wind, and goes forward, forward, forward, and never stops."

Sr. Teresa Forcades i Vila is a physician, theologian, and Benedictine nun at the mountain monastery of St. Benet de Montserrat in Catalonia, Spain.

Martyrdom

Bishop Borys Gudziak

Speaking in his house chapel in the Vatican on January 30, 2017, Pope Francis declared: "A church without martyrs . . . is a church without Jesus." As with many issues, when he identifies the church of Christ with martyrdom the Holy Father challenges predispositions of the modern world. In doing so he is in continuity with his predecessors. Where is the crux of the issue? In the modern West, the theme of martyrdom has commonly provoked discomfort or even embarrassment. This is not merely because contemporary suicide bombers and their maniacal carnage warp the profound and sacred meaning of the term. Derived from Greek and coming to us through Latin, *martyr* etymologically means "witness"—one who professes and manifests a salvific truth in the face of threats of violence, as did Christ himself. A martyr imitates the Lord in self-sacrifice, in giving his or her very life out of love for God and for God's truth. Tertullian's axiomatic and empirical tenet that "the blood of martyrs is seed for Christians" was fundamental for the church from Golgotha and the stoning of Stephen, from the original apostles and victims of the Roman Colosseum and imperial circuses to the martyr-missionaries of all ages and continents, the Gulag, and Auschwitz. Martyrdom is powerful. For the church and for the spiritual life of its faithful the death of martyrs, paradoxically, is life-giving.

Yet somehow martyrdom came to be marginalized even in Christian imagination, identity, and discourse. In a sense, the topic was relegated to a cruel and primitive past, ancient or medieval, one superseded by the enlightened ideals and epitomes of a rational age. One meets this attitude often—in academia, in polite company, but also in the church. In recent decades in Rome the ancient custom of stational liturgy and pilgrimage to the sites and "station" churches of the martyrs in the Eternal City has largely lapsed, with the exception of the practice of some Anglophones, mostly American clergy and seminarians. Correspondingly, when the post-communist Ukrainian Catholic University chose the *martyrs* and *marginalized* ("the two M's") as the twin pillars of its revived post–Soviet identity, one cardinal asked why the focus on a dour theme in a community of young people who want to live, overcome a genocidal, totalitarian past, and enjoy life.

Such unease is understandable. Martyrdom is *not* easy, enjoyable, or amusing—not as an ideal, not as an experience, not as a subject for reflection. Being killed by vicious persecutors is as a rule excruciatingly painful. But in today's *Weltanschauung* that puts a premium on pleasure, pain is to be avoided at all costs. We honour heroes, but there is cognitive dissonance between our respect for their sacrifice and our immersion in a therapeutic culture with its wellness wisdom and hedonistic proclivity. For the sceptic or pragmatist, atheist, or agnostic, martyrdom is, on the whole, "irrational" and nonsensical. For most people, it seems remote and obscure.

In teaching the recent history of the Ukrainian Greek Catholic Church—when it was brutally banned, constituting the largest illegal church in the world—I often sensed that I really was not "getting through" to UCU students about their own history. Two generations earlier, from the 1940s to the 1970s, many students and faculty of our school, who had sat in classrooms very much like ours, were martyred. Eight of them were beatified in 2001 by St. John Paul II. This registered at best as a historical fact but not as a future possibility or, for Christianity, a necessary modality. Yet, in 2014, it again became a UCU reality when our twenty-eight-year-old history lecturer, Bohdan Solchanyk, a fearless defender of civil liberties, was shot down by government snipers in the main square of Kyiv along with nearly a hundred other peaceful demonstrators—lambs who went to slaughter. Bohdan's witness to human dignity and that of the so-called "Heavenly Hundred" captivated the attention of the world and changed the course of Ukraine's history. The potency of the paschal sacrifice came alive for a whole nation. Something similar happened for Catholics in France with the slaying at the altar of Jacques Hamel, an elderly priest who was serving Mass at his parish in Saint-Étienne-du-Rouvray.

The radical nature of martyrdom and its meaning for the church, at all times and in all places, is ultimately eradicable. ISIS, al-Shabaab, Boko Haram, and scores of other Islamist terrorist formations remind us of this almost daily from Somalia, Sudan, Eritrea, Ethiopia, Nigeria, Libya, Egypt, and France to Syria, Iraq, Afghanistan, Pakistan, and Indonesia. There is enduring and sometimes brutal persecution of Christians in totalitarian or authoritarian states such as North Korea, Iran, Saudi Arabia, Uzbekistan, Vietnam, China, Turkey, and Kazakhstan. Christians face dangers in essentially democratic states such as India and Bangladesh. Non-Orthodox confessions face increasing pressure in Russia. In fact, more than half of the world's population lives in countries that do not guarantee full religious freedom to their citizens. Christians who confront economic exploitation, unjust politicians and their policies that keep tens of millions in grinding poverty, or denounce drug-running criminals have been brutally slain in Mexico, Colombia, and many Central and South American countries. It follows that in our day Christians can be martyred almost anywhere, any time. Martyrdom is remote until it becomes immediate.

To remedy modernity's negligence and misgivings, a fresh, traditional, and yet contemporary understanding of martyrdom was fostered by St. Pope John Paul II, whose theological vision was sustained and enhanced by Cardinal Joseph Ratzinger, the future Benedict XVI. In preparation for the new millennium, the pope from beyond the Iron Curtain, who himself saw the ultimate sacrifice of Christians at close hand, commended to all Catholics and people of good will the witness of martyrs not only of the early church but of all ages, especially of the twentieth century. He emphasized repeatedly that the twentieth century, in fact, generated more martyrs than all the previous 1,900 years of Christian history.

An emphasis on the witness of martyrs is an important part of the message of Pope Francis. His pontificate, one marked by innovative pastoral solicitude, stunning and sometimes controversial expressions, and prophetic gestures, is intentionally a pontificate of witness. The theme of martyrdom, foundational for the faith and radically countercultural, recurs in the Holy Father's sermons in different contexts—in Egypt and Armenia, in the Balkans and on the Tiber Island in the centre of Rome—bringing together history and the present. He has spoken about martyrdom to survivors of malicious attacks on Christians, to relatives of martyrs, the young, Catholics and non-Catholics, to all people of good will numbed by violence against believers. Francis has elucidated the darkness of suffering and the inherent connection between Christ's *pascha* and the trials and triumph of martyrdom to those who know suffering. He has also brought out the meaning and fruits of sacrifice for God and the faith to those who neither know nor understand them.

As the Year of Mercy demonstrated, Pope Francis seeks to highlight the radical love of God for humanity and the deep and often paradoxical truth of this love—God becomes small to be close to his creatures. As St. Athanasius said: "God had become man so that man could become God." The Son of God gives his life so that we could live. The path of the martyr is a trajectory of the Son of God who goes down—from heaven to earth, to Hades, hell itself—the place and condition of human torment. He descends from eternal glory to human suffering, to death on the cross. The Spirit of God guides and grows the church, "but the witness of Christians is necessary too. And when historical situations require a strong witness, there are martyrs, the greatest witnesses. And the church grows thanks to the blood of the martyrs. This is the beauty of martyrdom. It begins with witness, day after day, and it can end like Jesus, the first martyr, the first witness, the faithful witness: with blood" (homily, June 30, 2014). In his most important exhortation Francis wrote: "The disciple is ready to put his or her whole life on the line, even to accepting martyrdom, in bearing witness to Jesus Christ, yet the goal is not to make enemies but to see God's word accepted and its capacity for liberation and renewal revealed" (*Evangelii Gaudium* 24).

Like St. John Paul II, Pope Francis disabuses us of the notion that the Age of Martyrs is an ancient, past phenomenon: "There are more witnesses, more martyrs in the church today than there were in the first centuries." He stresses that martyrdom is not marginal in the life of the church: "A Christian who does not take seriously the 'martyrial' dimension of life has not understood the path Jesus taught us, the path of the martyrdom of daily life: the martyr's path of defending the rights of others; the martyr's path of defending one's children, of fathers and mothers who defend their families; the martyr's path of many, many sick people who suffer for love of Jesus" (speech at Coptic Orthodox Patriarchate,

M

Cairo, April 28, 2017). These examples help us to understand that "a martyr, in fact, is not one who remains relegated to the past, a lovely image that adorns our churches, and that we remember with a certain nostalgia. No, a martyr is a brother, a sister, who continues to accompany us in the mystery of the communion of saints and who, united to Christ, is not indifferent to our earthly pilgrimage, to our suffering, to our pain" (speech to pilgrims from El Salvador, October 30, 2015).

Does death and only death make a martyr? In Pope Francis's explanation, daily martyrdom, witnessing in day-to-day life is important along with ultimate sacrifice. At a prayer service honouring the martyrs of the twentieth and twenty-first centuries, Pope Francis asked, "How often, in difficult moments of history, have we heard it said: 'Today our country needs heroes?' Likewise, we can ask, 'Today what does our church need?' Martyrs, witnesses, that is, everyday saints of ordinary life, lives lived coherently; but we also need those who have the courage to accept the grace to be witnesses until the end, until death. All these are the living blood of the church" (April 22, 2017).

The strength of martyrdom makes manifest the truth of Christ's paschal suffering, because a martyr is the closest follower, imitator of Christ. People are transformed when they see authentic martyrdom. Recurrently in history the weak who lose their life become the heroes who overcome the pretentious and powerful. We, Ukrainian Greek Catholics, have seen how martyrs change history. We witnessed how the Soviet Union collapsed under the pressure of the love of martyrs. Martyrdom, to use the phrase of Vaclav Havel, is the "power of the powerless."

Such "overturning" is at the heart of Pope Francis's style. He reminds us of our sacred duty to remember our history, the legacy of our predecessors. Speaking to faithful in Sarajevo after hearing the testimonies of victims of communist persecution he said: "The witnesses' accounts speak for themselves. And this is the memory of your people! A people that forgets the past has no future. This is the memory of your fathers and mothers in the faith." The Holy Father continued: "You are blessed who have such witnesses so close to you: Do not forget them, please. Your life will grow with this memory" (June 6, 2015). We try not to forget. The Institute of Church History of the Ukrainian Catholic University gathered thousands of testimonies of witness and martyrdom from the Soviet period—not merely as archival artefacts, but as golden pages in a manual of how to maintain God-given human dignity in seemingly impossible circumstances.

Finally, Pope Francis emphasizes that martyrdom unites. In different circumstances, he has spoken about the ecumenism of blood. "Just as in the early church the shedding of the blood of martyrs became the seed of new Christians, so today the blood of the many martyrs of all the churches has become the seed of Christian unity" (Meeting with patriarch of the Ethiopian Orthodox Tewahedo Church, February 29, 2016). We are united in the blood of Christ and in blood of martyrs, those radical imitators of Christ.

The unease surrounding the theme of martyrdom is natural and widespread. Pope Francis speaks to it directly and encourages us to critically examine what it conceals. The difficulty of moderns and postmoderns regarding martyrdom is in fact a difficulty with the Gospel itself. We began in asking where is the crux of the issue. The crux is, in fact, in the cross itself and Christ's invitation to follow him on the way that leads to the Resurrection. It is sacrifice that gives life, selfless love that unifies and celebrates God's eternal truth no matter the price in the here and now. **M**

Bishop Borys Gudziak is the bishop of the Ukrainian Eparchy of St. Volodymyr the Great for France, Benelux and Switzerland, head of the Department of External Church Relations for the Ukrainian Greek Catholic Church, and president of the Ukrainian Catholic University in Lviv, Ukraine.

Mercy

Archbishop Donald Bolen

It did not take long for mercy to emerge as the central theme in Pope Francis's pontificate. In his Angelus address the first Sunday after being elected pope, he spoke of God's face as "the face of a merciful father" who "never ever tires of forgiving us." He commended a book he had just read, Cardinal Walter Kasper's *Mercy*, noting that mercy is "the best thing we can feel: it changes the world . . . changes everything . . . makes the world less cold and more just." Two years later he surprised the church by calling for an extraordinary Jubilee, a year with "the mercy of God at its centre," a year to be "steeped in mercy," so that "the balm of mercy [might] reach everyone" (*Misericordiae Vultus* 5, 25).

Pope Francis speaks of mercy as being at the heart of Christian faith, revealed most clearly in the incarnation and paschal mystery of Jesus. In a way analogous to how St. John, after expounding in so many ways on the love of God, finally tells us that "God *is* love" (1 John 4:8; italics added), Pope Francis speaks in numerous ways about how mercy takes us to the heart of the relationship between God and human beings, then states that mercy "is the name of God himself" (*The Name of God is Mercy*, 7). Reflecting on Psalm 136 and its constant repetition that God's mercy "endures forever," he notes that the refrain "seems to break through the dimensions of space and time, inserting everything into the eternal mystery of love. It is as if to say that not only in history, but for all eternity man will always be under the merciful gaze of the Father" (MV 7). Loving mercy is at the very foundation of creation and redemption.

God's Tender Mercies

The Father's mercy, shown in various ways to the people of Israel and throughout history, is revealed in a definitive way in Jesus. Jesus is the incarnation of God's creating and redeeming love. He is "mercy made flesh," "the face of the Father's mercy" (MV 24.1; NGM, 7). In Pope Francis's Christmas homilies, or when preaching about the incarnation, he stresses the great tenderness revealed in God's willingness to become small for us, to be near us especially in our struggles: "God immerses himself in our miseries, he approaches our wounds and heals them with his hands; it was to have hands that he became human." God saves us with his life given for us, "with tenderness, with caresses" (homily, October 22, 2013). His homily on Christmas Eve 2013 contains this simple prayer: "We bless you, Lord God most high, who lowered yourself for our sake. You are immense, and you made yourself small; you are rich and you made yourself poor; you are all-powerful and you made yourself vulnerable."

Jesus' mission was none other than to reveal the mystery of God's love in its fullness; in him God comes in search of us. Jesus' teaching, his deeds and signs, especially those reaching out to "sinners, the poor, the marginalized, the sick, and the suffering, are all meant to teach mercy. Everything in him speaks of mercy. Nothing in him is devoid of compassion" (MV 8). In fact, Pope Francis defines the Gospel as "the book of God's mercy, to be read and reread, because everything that Jesus said and did is an expression of the Father's mercy" (homily, April 3, 2016).

It is above all in Jesus' dying and rising that we learn that God's love "is never exhausted and it never gives up. There we see his infinite and boundless self-giving" (homily, June 3, 2016). Pope Francis's homilies and teachings on the paschal mystery are a creative invitation to see Jesus' dying and rising through the lens of God's mercy. On the cross, as Jesus "endured in his own flesh the dramatic encounter of the sin of the world and God's mercy," his words to his mother Mary and his disciple John, and his response to those who crucified him, reveal "a love that bestows itself without limits," "a mercy that accepts and forgives everything" (*Evangelii Gaudium* 285; homily, June 12, 2016).

At the Easter Vigil of 2017, Pope Francis related how it was precisely when it seemed, with Jesus' death, that the final word had been spoken, that "God suddenly breaks in, upsets all the rules and offers new possibilities. God once more comes to meet us, to create and consolidate a new age, the age of mercy. This is the promise present from the beginning." In other words, it had been about mercy from the start; our creation, our history, human life, had always been about God's desire to redeem us by his merciful gift of self.

Resurrection hope is not a naïve optimism, but rather, the work of the Holy Spirit in us. The Holy Spirit, the supreme gift of the crucified and risen Christ, pours out "a vast torrent of grace" upon humanity, bringing forgiveness, the possibility of living in hope as brothers and sisters, and the summons to witness to God's great mercy towards us (Pentecost, May 15, 2016). At the Easter Vigil of 2016, Pope Francis noted that the Paraclete "does not remove evil with a magic wand. But he pours into us the vitality of life, which is not the absence of problems, but the certainty of being loved and always forgiven by Christ, who for us has conquered sin, conquered death and conquered fear." The Spirit allows us to face directly life's problems and illnesses, our world's wars and tragedies, and not be overwhelmed by them, because nothing is outside the reach of the resurrection.

In *Evangelii Gaudium*, Pope Francis offers a concise expression of the apostolic *kerygma*, the core trinitarian proclamation of the church which is to be "the centre of all evangelizing activity and all efforts at Church renewal": the Holy Spirit leads us to believe in and proclaim "Jesus Christ who, by his death and resurrection, reveals and communicates to us the Father's infinite mercy" (EG 164). Pope Francis is at pains to show that this message, with mercy at the very heart of it, is not new. He quotes the Old Testament and the New, patristic authors, Augustine, Aquinas, and recent popes on mercy. But *there is something new here*, a new emphasis, a creative and strong proclamation of mercy that resounds from his pontificate. One gets the sense that he would be stumbling for words without it, and at the same time he loads it with meaning as vast and comprehensive as God's relationship with humanity.

Forgiveness, Love, Justice and Mercy

When Pope Francis speaks of mercy, it is often in terms of God's profound desire to pour down forgiveness upon us. Near the beginning of *Evangelii Gaudium*, he urges that "now is the time to say to Jesus: 'Lord, I have let myself be deceived; in a thousand ways I have shunned your love, yet here I am once more, to renew my covenant with you. I need you. Save

me once again, Lord, take me once more into your redeeming embrace.'
. . . God never tires of forgiving us; we are the ones who tire of seeking
his mercy" (EG 3). Such references are a major part of his preaching and
teaching, and the focus is not so much on the sin of the past, as on God's
concern for our future. To prisoners, he stated, "let us never yield to the
temptation of thinking that we cannot be forgiven" (homily, November
6, 2016); to those in organized crime or involved in corruption, "this
is the opportune moment to change our lives!" (MV 19). God joyfully
pardons us, and such mercy is transformative; it announces a new season
in our lives. "God has no memory of sin, but only of us, of each of us, we
who are his beloved children. And he believes that it is always possible
to start anew" (homily, November 20, 2016). Forgiveness is essential for
building community, for holding us together. A gift of the Holy Spirit, it
"is gift to the highest degree; it is the greatest love of all. It preserves unity
despite everything, prevents collapse, and consolidates and strengthens."
Forgiveness brings freedom, hope and joy.

Yet mercy is not only a response to human sin; it is, more generally,
God's tender and compassionate response to the human condition in all
its complexity, brokenness, and beauty. Mercy is not in the first instance
a love between equals, but the love of the Creator for those created in his
image and likeness. It is a love that creates, heals, and makes things whole.
Pope Francis ended the Jubilee Year of Mercy on the feast of Christ the
King, proclaiming: "Christ lowered himself to us out of this love, he lived
our human misery, he suffered the lowest point of our human condition:
injustice, betrayal, abandonment; he experienced death, the tomb, hell.
And so our King went to the ends of the universe in order to embrace and
save every living being. . . . His rule of love transforms sin into grace,
death into resurrection, fear into trust" (homily, November 20, 2016).
Mercy is the shape God's love takes when responding to human beings.

Pope Francis addresses at length the relationship between mercy and
justice. The discussion might best be framed by the disproportion between
the self-giving suffering love of God by which we are redeemed, and
what we deserve as a result of our actions. God "believes in us, infinitely
beyond any merits we have" (homily, November 20, 2016); "no human
efforts, however good they may be, can enable us to merit so great a gift"
as salvation given through God's mercy (EG 112). Justice and mercy "are
not two contradictory realities, but two dimensions of a single reality"

flowing from God's loving desire not to condemn but to redeem us. Pope Francis notes that when Jesus was faced with a vision of justice that was limited to a formal respect for the law and that labelled people either as "the just" or "sinners," he challenged it in practice by reaching out to the margins, and summoning his disciples to "place mercy at the centre."

Justice and mercy meet most intimately on the cross of Christ. The cross "is God's judgment on all of us and on the whole world," and it is there above all that God's mercy is revealed, in an action that justifies us despite our guilt. Pope Francis is not espousing the cheap grace that Dietrich Bonhoeffer famously criticized. God asks something of us, and we are accountable to God; justice is not devalued or rendered superfluous. But in the ministry of Jesus, in his costly gift of self on the cross, and in his resurrection, we witness that for God justice is not enough; justice won't offer us the kingdom, and that's what God desires to offer us. Grappling to give words to this saving mystery, Pope Francis notes: "God goes beyond justice with his mercy and forgiveness"; "God's justice is his mercy given to everyone as a grace that flows from the death and resurrection of Jesus Christ" (MV 20–21).

Proclamation, Witness, and Transformation

The American writer Annie Dillard, in her book *Pilgrim at Tinker Creek*, uses a hope-filled image: "I feel as though I stand at the foot of an infinitely high staircase, down which some exuberant spirit is flinging tennis ball after tennis ball, eternally, and the one thing I want in the world is a tennis ball" (p. 102). Analogously, Pope Francis looks at the world around him, and assesses that the one thing people of today need is mercy. In addition to the myriad ways in which we get stuck in sin and are lost or astray, he also addresses with great frequency those who are trafficked, the refugees, the victims of war and violence, the wounded who are without dignity, those crushed by poverty, the unemployed, those burdened by sorrow, the spiritually adrift, those in broken relationships—in sum, "the misery of the world" (MV 15). This is the world in need of mercy, in order to find the courage to continue to live, to hope, to find joy.

The Good News is that God offers to the world precisely what it most needs and longs for, if we only avail ourselves of it. "From the depths of the mystery of God, the great river of mercy wells up and overflows unceasingly. It is a spring that will never run dry, no matter how many people approach it. Every time someone is in need, he or she can approach it, because the mercy of God never ends" (MV 25).

For Pope Francis, the church's mission is thus to show the mercy that has been shown to us. "Jesus affirms that mercy is not only an action of the Father, it becomes a criterion for ascertaining who his true children are. In short, we are called to show mercy because mercy has first been shown to us. . . . As the Father loves, so do his children. Just as he is merciful, so we are called to be merciful to each other" (MV 9). We who have encountered God's mercy are called to become "instruments of mercy" (MV 14) in our proclamation, our witness, and by being transformed ourselves.

The church's "primary task" is "to introduce everyone to the great mystery of God's mercy by contemplating the face of Christ"; to be "a convincing herald of mercy" (MV 25). "What we say and how we say it, our every word and gesture, ought to express God's compassion, tenderness and forgiveness for all" (message, World Day of Communications, 2016). Pope Francis cites St. Pope John Paul II in saying that "the Church lives an authentic life when she professes and proclaims mercy—the most stupendous attribute of the Creator and of the Redeemer—and when she brings people close to the sources of the Savior's mercy, of which she is the trustee and dispenser" (MV 11 citing *Dives in Misericordia* 13). The church proclaims God's mercy—"the beating heart of the Gospel"—in its preaching and in its sacraments (MV 12). During the Jubilee Year, Pope Francis gave particular attention to the sacrament of reconciliation, encouraging confessors to model themselves after the father in the parable of the Prodigal Son, who rushes out to meet and welcome the prodigal despite his sin. The confessional "must not be a torture chamber," but a place of encounter with God's mercy (EG 44). "In short, confessors are called to be a sign of the primacy of mercy always, everywhere, and in every situation, no matter what" (MV 17).

The church's proclamation of mercy is made credible by its witness. Pope Francis extends a great challenge here: "Perhaps we have long since forgotten how to show and live the way of mercy" (MV 10). The Jubilee Year was to be "a time for the Church to rediscover the meaning of the mission entrusted to her by the Lord on the day of Easter: to be a sign and an instrument of the Father's mercy" (homily, April 11, 2015). All of the church's pastoral activity "should be caught up in the tenderness she makes present to believers"; mercy is to be "the distinctive trait of all that she is and does" (MV 10; message for 2016 World Day of Communication). God's immense generosity, the free gift of himself in mercy, needs to be made concrete and tangible in the life of the church, as gift for the world.

While witnessing to God's mercy is comprehensive of the church living its mission, Pope Francis points our attention more generally to the corporal and spiritual works of mercy, which are hallmarks of faithful discipleship, reawakening our consciences and reminding us that "faith finds expression in concrete everyday actions meant to help our neighbours in body and spirit" (Message for Lent 2016). More specifically and passionately, he summons the church to draw near to people in their wounds, to "return to the basics and to bear the weaknesses and struggles of our brothers and sisters" (MV 10). "In life, God accompanies people, and we must accompany them, starting from their situation. It is necessary to accompany them with mercy. . . . The ministers of the church must be ministers of mercy above all" (2013 interview with Fr. Antonio Spadaro). Mercy seeks out those who are suffering or struggling, to bandage the wounds and bring healing. Pope Francis notes that "God shows the poor 'his first mercy'" (EG 198). Inspired by God's decision to become poor for us in Jesus, and by Jesus' ministry of outreach, the church "has made an option for the poor which is understood as a 'special form of primacy in the exercise of Christian charity' (citing St. Pope John Paul II, *Sollicitudo Rei Socialis* 42). . . . This is why I want a Church which is poor and for the poor," a community of disciples that "is willing to abase itself if necessary, . . . embrac[ing] human life, touching the suffering flesh of Christ in others" (EG 198; 24).

The strongest witness the church can give is that it be transformed by the gospel of mercy it proclaims. Mercy is God's way of changing the world, transforming us, that the world might be transformed. Pope Francis is conscious that as a community of disciples, we will fail again and again in our efforts to proclaim and live that message with integrity, and we will repeatedly need to rediscover for ourselves the mercy of God. Along the way, Pope Francis summons us to prayer, contemplating "the face of mercy" in Jesus; to read and study the Scriptures, which open us to the Father's mercy; and to draw on our own memories, recalling "how we have received mercy" in order to commit ourselves, day in and day out, to be artisans of mercy (homily, November 20, 2016). That transformation is communal, but also intensely personal, as each of us must continue to come home to the place where we encounter the heart of the Good Shepherd, a heart that not only "shows us mercy, but *is* itself mercy. . . . There I know I am welcomed and understood as I am; there, with all my sins and limitations, I know the certainty that I am chosen and loved. Contemplating that heart, I renew my first love: the memory of that time when the Lord touched my soul and called me to follow him" (homily, June 3, 2016).

"Mercy within Mercy within Mercy"

That last reference, remembering the moment of being chosen and loved, brings to mind Pope Francis's episcopal motto: *miserando atque eligendo*. Taken from St. Bede, it speaks about the call of Matthew. It is not easy to translate, but communicates that Jesus looked on Matthew with mercy and called him. The choosing of an episcopal motto is a personal matter; you ask yourself what phrase is going to take people to the heart of what you are trying to live and proclaim. When I was named a bishop in 2009 and prayed about this, a phrase from Thomas Merton's *The Sign of Jonas* laid hold of my imagination. Merton had God saying to Jonah: "I have always overshadowed Jonas with My mercy, and cruelty I know not at all. Have you had sight of Me, Jonas My child? Mercy within mercy within mercy." When I proposed "mercy within mercy within mercy" to heraldic authorities as my motto, I was encouraged to drop one "within mercy" as it was "a little redundant." I held firm. When interviewed by a Jesuit confrere soon after his election as pope, the Holy Father spoke about his motto in responding to a question about his deepest identity, referring to Caravaggio's painting of the call of St. Matthew: "That finger of Jesus, pointing at Matthew. That's me. I feel like him. Like Matthew. . . . Here, this is me, a sinner on whom the Lord has turned his gaze. And this is what I said when they asked me if I would accept my election as pontiff. . . . I am a sinner, but I trust in the infinite mercy and patience of our Lord Jesus Christ, and I accept in a spirit of penance" (2013 interview with Fr. Antonio Spadaro).

Pope Francis is clearly leading the church out of his own experience that God has looked upon him in his need, loved him, and called him. And he trusts that God looks upon each and all of us with that same mercy. In closing the Jubilee of Mercy, he invited us to "entrust the life of the Church, all humanity, and the entire cosmos to the Lordship of Christ, asking him to pour out his mercy upon us like the morning dew, so that everyone may work together to build a brighter future" (homily, November 20, 2016). Trusting in God's tender mercies, may it ever be so.

Archbishop Donald Bolen leads the Archdiocese of Regina, Saskatchewan, Canada. He is the Catholic co-chair of the International Anglican–Roman Catholic Commission on Unity and Mission and a member of the Pontifical Council for Promoting Christian Unity.

Miracles

John Thavis

Two months after his election in 2013, Pope Francis tweeted: "Miracles happen. But prayer is needed! Prayer that is courageous, struggling and persevering, not prayer that is a mere formality."

It was an unusual proclamation by a pope who has brought a distinctive and down-to-earth approach to miracles, apparitions, and all things supernatural in the Catholic Church. When it comes to the other-worldly, the Latin American pontiff sometimes sounds like a traditionalist. He warns about the influence of the devil, turns to Mary for spiritual advice, and believes the saints intercede on our behalf. He once told stunned reporters that when he prays to St. Thérèse of Lisieux, he "almost always" receives a rose in response—a tangible sign that those in heaven are listening.

Yet Pope Francis has cautioned the faithful against excessive "sign-seeking" and expressed his personal scepticism about some Marian apparitions and messages. For him, it's a question of balance: the demands of the Gospel in this world should never be overshadowed by mystical melodrama.

"God doesn't work like a fairy with a magic wand," the pope said early in his pontificate.

A corollary might be that the devil doesn't work with smoke and sulphur.

The pope's frequent references to Satan have surprised many observers. He characterizes the devil as a sly charmer who often comes "disguised as an angel," requiring a spiritual discernment like that practised by St. Ignatius of Loyola, the founder of the pope's own Jesuit order. For Pope Francis, the devil is a real person and not merely symbolic or allegorical. "On this point there is no shadow of a doubt," he says. "A battle exists, a battle in which the eternal salvation of us all is at stake." But this is not the Satan of *The Exorcist*, who possesses people violently against their will or makes their heads spin around. In the pope's view, the devil is much more clever: a con artist and a manipulator, an evil spirit who "infects" human relationships with gossip, jealousy, and moral compromises.

This attention to the practical over the theatrical has characterized encounters between Pope Francis and some of the church's most sacred icons and relics. When he venerated the Shroud of Turin, believed by many to be the burial cloth of the crucified Christ, he steered clear of the debate over its authenticity, which has fascinated scientists and believers for centuries. Instead, the pope said Christians should reflect on the image and draw inspiration to help the suffering in their midst.

The pope's visit to Naples in 2015 brought him face-to-face with a relic that, at least in local belief, has worked miracles and saved the city from disaster: the blood of St. Januarius. As Pope Francis stood before the altar, the Neapolitan archbishop held the reliquary aloft and announced that the saint's blood had begun to liquefy in the pope's presence, prompting cries of "Miracolo!" among the faithful. The pope's response? He cracked a joke and then quickly left the cathedral for a meeting with the sick and disabled.

The pope often shows his deep and personal devotion to Mary and speaks openly about seeking her counsel. Yet unlike his predecessors, he has bluntly cautioned against reading too much into alleged Marian apparitions and messages, saying that it reflects an unhealthy "spirit of curiosity" that can lead people astray. Visiting the Portuguese sanctuary of Fatima in 2017, the pope marked the hundredth anniversary of Mary's apparitions there and canonized two of the three visionaries who, as small children, reported seeing the Madonna and receiving messages from her. Yet the pope refused to be drawn into the longstanding debate over the interpretation of the enigmatic Fatima messages, preferring to emphasize Mary's message of peace and her special love for the poor, the sick, and the abandoned.

On his plane returning to Rome from Fatima, reporters asked the pope about the alleged apparitions in Medjugorje, a town in Herzegovina where Mary has reportedly been appearing daily since 1981, drawing an estimated 35 million pilgrims. A Vatican-appointed commission studied Medjugorje for several years, but Pope Francis has waited to reveal its recommendations. On the plane, the pope praised the commission for its good work and spoke of the many conversions at Medjugorje, saying the church needs to provide pastoral care to the pilgrims there. But he also noted doctrinal doubts about the apparitions and offered what he called a "personal opinion" that struck a nerve among many Medjugorje devotees: "I prefer Our Lady to be a mother, our mother, and not a telegraph operator who sends out a message every day at a certain time. This is not the mother of Jesus. And these alleged apparitions have no great value," he said. His comments reflected deep concern that Catholics who obsess over supposedly divine messages risk losing touch with the real-life issues of the faith.

As for miracles, the pope believes in them, and he believes in the power of prayer. He once recounted the story of a Buenos Aires man whose seven-year-old daughter was given a few hours to live. The man drove for hours to the Marian sanctuary of Luján and spent the entire night praying to Mary and "struggling with God" over the girl's fate. When he returned to the hospital the next morning, he found his daughter healed. "Miracles happen," the pope concluded, but they require dedication and sometimes suffering. They cannot be summoned on demand, and they are usually a response to a lifetime of spiritual activity rather than a perfunctory appeal to God, he said.

Pope Francis says the greatest miracles are often acts of reconciliation, forgiveness and conversion—all of which demand spiritual effort. "God saves us in time, not in the moment. Sometimes he performs miracles, but in ordinary life, he saves us in time. The Lord comes into our life and changes us, that's what conversion is. But this change has to develop, it has to make history."

John Thavis covered the Vatican for 30 years for Catholic News Service. His latest book is The Vatican Prophecies: Investigating Supernatural Signs, Apparitions and Miracles in the Modern Age.

Money

Andrea Tornielli

There is a word that comes up repeatedly in Pope Francis's preaching, his use of which has even prompted some to accuse him of being a "Marxist" or a "Leninist." It is the word *money*, or as he calls it, "the god of money," which he insists "must serve, not rule." The pope says that when money rules, when it is idolized, adored, put first of all and above all, it corrupts people. Many have wished to anaesthetize and explain away the meaning of Francis's words on this subject, saying that the pope talks like he does because he comes from Latin America and therefore looks at the world with the eyes of a South American who does not understand the economy. In reality, though, Francis's preaching helps us rediscover forgotten pages of the church's social teaching, as well as those of the early church fathers.

For Pope Francis, when money is worshiped it weakens faith. "It is the power of money that makes you deviate from authentic faith. It cuts you off from the faith, and weakens you so that you lose it," he said in his September 20, 2013, morning homily. He said money sows "jealousy, quarrels, bad feelings, suspicions" in the world. "If you choose the way of money, in the end you will end up corrupt." And the pope reminded us that Jesus himself spoke clearly on this, in strong words: "[Jesus said,] 'You cannot serve both God and money.' It can't be done. It must be one or the other. And this is not communism. This is the pure Gospel. These are the words of Jesus."

Francis also offered clear words on the topic in *Evangelii Gaudium*, the 2013 apostolic exhortation that has become the road map of his pontificate. There he wrote: "The worship of the ancient golden calf (cf. Ex 32:1-35) has returned in a new and ruthless guise in the idolatry of money and the dictatorship of an impersonal economy lacking a truly human purpose" (EG 55). He added: "Such an economy kills" (EG 53).

Since *Evangelii Gaudium*'s publication, Francis's strong words have come under fire by critics, especially those associated with organizations—even some Catholic ones—who would have us believe that capitalism and the Christian faith are a perfect match. They consider the current economic–financial system to be the best of all possible worlds, almost a systematization of the Christian vision of the human person. These think tanks, alarmed by the pope's preaching, dismiss Francis's words as an expression of a populist mentality. But they forget that the Argentina in which Jorge Mario Bergoglio was born and lived experienced the adverse consequences of the 2008 financial crisis and of a certain neoliberalism nearly a decade ahead of the rest of the Western world. Witnessing this firsthand as archbishop of Buenos Aires, Cardinal Bergoglio retrieved the strong and prophetic words of Pope Pius XI, who in his 1931 encyclical *Quadragesimo Anno*—published two years after the start of the Great **M** Depression—spoke of an "international imperialism whose country is where profit is" (QA 109).

"In the first place," Pius XI taught, "it is obvious that not only is wealth concentrated in our times but an immense power and despotic economic dictatorship is consolidated in the hands of a few, who often are not owners but only the trustees and managing directors of invested funds which they administer according to their own arbitrary will and pleasure" (QA 105). It was all there already, an incisive reading of the present moment, in that now forgotten encyclical.

In a 2002 interview with the Italian magazine *30 Giorni*, Bergoglio recalled Pius XI's words, observing:

> The teaching never loses its relevance and has biblical roots. When Moses ascended the mountain to receive God's law, the people embraced the sin of idolatry by making the golden calf. The present imperialism of money shows the same unmistakable idolatrous face. It is curious how idolatry always comes together with gold. And where there is idolatry, God and the dignity of humanity, made in God's image, are erased. The speculative economy no longer has need

of work, it doesn't know what to do with work. It follows the idol of money that it produces by itself. That's why it does not hesitate to transform millions of workers into unemployed people.

It should be unnecessary to point out that neither the Catholic Church nor this Argentine pope has anything against wealth, and they do not condemn free enterprise and capitalism per se. Francis was clear on this point in an interview he gave to Giacomo Galeazzi and me for our book *This Economy Kills: Pope Francis on Capitalism and Social Justice*. The pope stated:

> Poverty protects us from idolatry, from self-sufficiency. Zacchaeus, after meeting Jesus' merciful gaze, donated half of his possessions to the poor. The Gospel message is for all; the Gospel does not condemn the rich but the idolatry of wealth, that idolatry that makes us insensitive to the cry of the poor. Jesus said that before offering our gift at the altar we must reconcile ourselves with our brother and sister to be at peace with him. I believe that, by analogy, we can also extend this request to being at peace with our poor brothers and sisters.

It must be said, in the face of certain reactions to the pope's social teaching, that the problem is not his words but rather Christians who have forgotten the power of the church's social doctrine or have watered down its message. In his view of money, wealth, and sharing with the poor, Pope Francis knows that he is in good company with the early church fathers. Later in our interview for *This Economy Kills*, he stated:

> If I repeated some passages from the homilies of the early fathers of the church—say, of the second or third century—about how we should treat the poor, there would certainly be someone saying that my homily is Marxist. "You are not making a gift of what is yours to the poor, but you are giving back what is theirs. You have been appropriating things that are meant to be for the common use of everyone. The earth belongs to everyone, not to the rich." These are St. Ambrose's words, which Pope Paul VI cited in *Populorum Progressio* to affirm that private property does not constitute an absolute and unconditioned right for anyone and that, when others lack basic necessities, no one is justified in keeping for one's exclusive use what is not needed.

Pope Francis also borrows from the church fathers one of the strongest images he uses when speaking of money, describing it as "the dung of the devil." To the Second World Meeting of Popular Movements, held in Bolivia in 2015, the pope said:

> Today, the scientific community realizes what the poor have long told us: harm, perhaps irreversible harm, is being done to the ecosystem. The earth, entire peoples and individual persons are being brutally punished. And behind all this pain, death and destruction there is the stench of what Basil of Caesarea—one of the first theologians of the church—called "the dung of the devil." An unfettered pursuit of money rules. This is the "dung of the devil." The service of the common good is left behind. Once capital becomes an idol and guides people's decisions, once greed for money presides over the entire socioeconomic system, it ruins society, it condemns and enslaves men and women, it destroys human fraternity, it sets people against one another and, as we clearly see, it even puts at risk our common home, sister and mother earth.

In the face of all of this, in the face of the idolatry of money that is so widespread today, Francis calls us to a profound change and calls into question the system in which we live. The economy per se does not kill, but when money rules rather than serves, then "this economy kills."

One could argue that greed, the idolatry of money, this unhealthy attachment, have always existed. The Bible tells us of the golden calf, and Jesus himself was sold for thirty pieces of silver. But the novelty of our times is that this has all been transformed into a system. Francis goes beyond general, slogan-like criticisms of this. He describes its consequences in detail. During a visit to Genoa, Italy, in May 2017, Francis told a group of workers:

> One illness of our economy is the progressive transformation of entrepreneurs into speculators. The entrepreneur is not the same as the speculator; they are different. The speculator is a figure similar to what Jesus in the Gospel calls a mercenary, whom he contrasts with the good shepherd. He sees a business and its workers only as a means to profit and uses them to make a profit. He doesn't love them. The speculator doesn't hesitate to sell, close, or move the company, because he uses, exploits, eats people and means for profit. When

good entrepreneurs inhabit the economy, businesses are friends of the people. When speculators control it, everything is ruined. It is a faceless, abstract economy. There are no people behind the decisions of the speculator, and so one doesn't see the people who are doing the selling and the cutting.

Finally, it must not be forgotten that for Pope Francis the economic interests and the love of money contribute to the outbreak of war. What he has called the "piecemeal third world war" is a phenomenon that is being carried out today by the avid traffickers of death. "Why is it that so many powerful people don't want peace? Because they live on war!" Francis told a group of students in May 2015. "Some of the powerful profit from the production of arms and they sell arms to this country which is against that one, and then they sell them to the one that goes against this one. It is the industry of death! And they profit." A few months later, in his historic address to the US Congress in September 2015, he posed a rhetorical question: "Why are deadly weapons being sold to those who plan to inflict untold suffering on individuals and society? Sadly, the answer, as we all know, is simply for money: money that is drenched in blood, often innocent blood."

Andrea Tornielli is an Italian journalist who is a correspondent for the newspaper La Stampa *and director of the* Vatican Insider *news website. He has published many books on the history of the church and the Vatican and is the author of* The Name of God is Mercy, *a book-length interview with Pope Francis.*

Periphery

Carolyn Y. Woo

When Cardinal Jorge Mario Bergolio addressed the College of Cardinals before the papal election, he put into public discourse in the Catholic Church the concept of the "periphery." Since then, the call for the church to go out to the periphery and embrace this as our mission field has been integral to Pope Francis's core message. He reminds us that Jesus came from the periphery—being born in a shelter for animals, displaced with his parents as refugees, and raised in the backwater town of its time—and sought out those despised by the mainstream, including prostitutes, widows, tax collectors, and criminals.

In Pope Francis's urging, the periphery refers to all people who are excluded, forgotten, abandoned, shoved aside, and in the most vivid description "thrown away." Such exclusion takes place across many divides and includes refugees, those living in deep poverty, the elderly, people with disabilities, prisoners, and people who experience rejection by the church.

At a meeting in Bolivia in 2015, Pope Francis addressed members of intentional communities and cautioned against "an excess of paralysis" as well as the instinct to retreat to our small circles of friends and families when we face the enormity of the consequences from injustice, profits at all costs, human deprivations, and destruction of the earth. He made it a point that all of us, regardless of power and position, can do something. He noted, "You, dear brothers and sisters, often work on little things, in local situations, amid forms of injustice which you do not simply accept but actively resist, standing up to an idolatrous system which excludes, debases and kills."

Catholic Relief Services (CRS), the official humanitarian agency of the US Catholic Church, journeys to the periphery inhabited by the poorest and most vulnerable people outside of the United States. For almost seventy-five years, CRS has been reaching out to people in need regardless of creed so as to render in flesh the words of the parable of the Good Samaritan and alleviate the suffering of Christ who located himself in the least among us.

Except in the most devastating emergency situations, to truly serve the poor and vulnerable is not to "give away things" or simply transfer assets such as money, food, medicines, and so on. The mission is to address the root causes that leave people unable to prosper in their circumstances and meet basic needs that allow them to flourish. Often, the causes stem from a lack of access to key resources such as knowledge, tools, quality inputs, infrastructure, information, markets, rights to land, and participation in governance. Outcomes are not just economic in nature, but multidimensional, as embodied in Catholic Social Teachings (CST) that specify the primacy of human life, necessity of human dignity, the appropriate rights to "land, lodging, labour" as Pope Francis identifies, cohesion of families and communities, solidarity with those who suffer, and care for the earth. Above all, the solutions must emanate from the local communities themselves in alignment with the CST principle of subsidiarity or self-determination by the affected people.

From my eleven years with CRS as a board and staff member, I see that the needed changes are no match for human ingenuity and genuine commitment. Effective and sustainable transformations have emerged when smallholder farmers, for example, have access to quality seeds, knowledge to plant alternative crops, growing methods that yield higher productivity, "green water management" mechanisms to access and retain as much moisture as possible in plants and soils, approaches to improve soil health, education and nutrition for their families, training that enables the formation of effective cooperatives and analysis of both crop health and markets, mediation skills that diffuse tensions and forge collaboration, the capacity to build local pools of savings, and a voice in local, regional, and national governance.

As Pope Francis has often taught, we are not to think of these brothers and sisters in the abstract, but rather we must encounter them and hold them in our hearts. Let me recall a few encounters from my years at CRS: the boy with a stomach the size of a soccer ball because it was impregnated with shrapnel; a migrant who was dropped in Mexico from Guatemala having paid a coyote his family's total savings to take him to the United States; and the young men from North Africa, the Middle East and Afghanistan in a Serbian park recovering from their beatings at the various European borders they tried to cross. I saw my two sons in them every time, and their suffering becomes unshakeable. They all had the same parting message: "Please do not let the world forget us."

I also have stories of human triumph from my encounters: the women in an El Salvador village who named their group "Intelligence" after they turned their land and households into fruitful enterprises, healthy homes, and joy-filled families; the Muslim refugee who named his newborn daughter "Caritas" as he settled into stable and fulfilling employment in his host country; and the woman in Lebanon who devoted her life to serving in a women's shelter and brought food to a prison on her days off. She was driven by unbounded gratitude for God's blessings after having lost a leg in an accident that resulted in her freedom from slavery as a trafficked person.

As Pope Francis puts the periphery into our mission, he cautions us not just to look at the world from the viewpoint of the core or the centre, but from the viewpoint of the people on the periphery. We are called to meet the world from their vantage point and not be complicit in a system that does not see them, register their children, or invest resources for their wellbeing. They see a world of opportunities but only for others as there are no paths, gates, or ladders visible or seemingly accessible to them. If at any time we start to cast people in the periphery as "the other," it is helpful to remember that they want the same things we do: the ability to flourish, provide for their families, see their children prosper, do meaningful work, live in peace, be counted, be welcomed, have some modicum of independence that enables dignity, and have a voice in decisions affecting them. Encounter, as theologian Karl Barth wrote, goes beyond beholding and listening, beyond being with the person, but being for the person, and to do so with a sense of joy. Otherwise it is merely a random meeting, not an encounter.

The most important message I believe we must listen hard for from the people in the periphery is not the stories of hardships, but the whispers of their dreams and their unspoken pride in what they stand to contribute. In a way, those of us who serve at the periphery are akin to talent agents who see what is possible and hear the passion behind these dreams. Subsidiarity, a key Catholic principle for serving at the periphery, is not just about soliciting input and feedback, forging self-determination or achieving inclusive governance. It is ultimately the recognition that the gifts of the people at the periphery with their individual talents, cultural heritages, religious practices, strong familial bonds, and commitment to each other are the pavers of new sustainable, dignifying core communities no longer at the periphery of other societies.

Dr. Carolyn Y. Woo is the retired CEO and president of Catholic Relief Services.

Prayer

Bishop Daniel E. Flores

I had Mass with Pope Francis at the Basilica of Our Lady of Guadalupe in Mexico City. Well, I and a couple of hundred thousand others in and around the basilica. There we were, from different places and coming with different concerns, the rich and the mighty poor, the communion of the baptized around the successor of Peter, at the altar of Christ in the house of the Virgin Mother of God. Here was the church on sacramental display, showing forth her identity as a body at prayer. This is what I first think about when asked about this pope and prayer.

I have only greeted Pope Francis briefly on a few occasions. But watching him celebrate Mass, hearing him preach, and being in his presence when he pauses for silent contemplation are experiences, like the one in Mexico City, that have left deep traces on my mind. Maybe in our individualized societies, with our relational selectivity, we think first about personal prayer when we use the word "prayer." But I think for the Holy Father, prayer is first of all a work initiated by the living God who swoops into our lives and pulls us into his vision and into his activity. The event of God's swooping is the creation of an "us," a people, a body. We are never more at prayer than when it is we who pray. This is why it came so naturally to Pope Francis to ask for the prayers and blessing of the great crowds assembled at St. Peter's Square on the night of his election. There is great grace and blessing in the assembly of the communion of the baptized. This is also why the eucharistic sacrifice is the clearest expression of what Christian prayer is about. "United to the Incarnate Son, present in the Eucharist, the whole cosmos gives thanks to God" (*Laudato Si'* 236).

Christians can pray because Christ Jesus speaks to us first. He started the manifest conversation in the physicality of his incarnation. Every word he utters in the Gospel is his petition to us for a response, a dialogue, an encounter. When the Holy Father preaches, he is showing us that prayer is a response to Jesus in the flesh. Not just to his words or to his teaching but to him in person: "Jesus wished to introduce his companions into the mystery of life, into the mystery of his life. . . . He invited them to share his life, his interiority, and in his presence among them he allowed them to touch, in his flesh, the life of the Father" (homily in Morelia, Michoacán, February 16, 2016).

Some have said that the Holy Father's preaching is down-to-earth, or even earthy. I would say that Pope Francis has the gift of getting to the point. The church is supposed to be like your mother, not your mother-in-law, he is said to have said once. Whether he did or did not say exactly that is not as important as the fact that we can all imagine that he *could* have said it. The Lord was fairly earthy in his preaching too: Jesus said in reply, "It is not right to take the food of the children and throw it to the dogs" (Matt 15:26). This is not exactly the saying of one whose first priority is politeness. Yet as with the Gospel itself, the abruptness and the imagery the pope uses all point to mercy. Only prayer can successfully navigate that kind of preacher's curve. "A preacher has to contemplate the Word, but he also has to contemplate his people" (*Evangelii Gaudium* 154).

Prayer cannot help but draw us into the paschal mystery. People have commented, and I have noticed, that when the pope celebrates Mass there is very little change in his facial expression. He is intensely present to the mystery, especially as he approaches the altar. And yet he is profoundly aware that he is not alone, that there is a throng around him. It is as if he wants us all to be present to Christ in his sacrifice and be aware of the many who are with us, and aware also of the many who are not with us. "The mystic experiences the intimate connection between God and all beings, and thus feels that 'all things are God'" (LS 234, quoting St. John of the Cross, Spiritual Canticle xiv–xv, 5).

As it is in the Mass, so it is also in our personal moments of prayer and communion with the Lord. To pray requires a steady gaze at Christ, rooted in the gospel text, one that sees in him and with him all others who are around us, living, breathing, suffering, and hoping. Thus, the Holy Father is unyieldingly insistent on giving voice to the plight of the poor, not because he is an activist but because he is a contemplative: "God's shrine is the life of his children, of everyone in whatever condition. . . . The shrine of God is the faces of the many people we encounter each day" (homily, Basilica of Our Lady of Guadalupe, Mexico City, February 13, 2016).

This is the kind of intensely focused gaze I have sensed when the Holy Father celebrates the Mass. It is also the gaze of his attention as he prays to the Mother of God. To try to explain the Holy Father's devotion to the Virgin Mother of God would be futile—and in some ways disrespectful. Love is love, and it resists being understood apart from our own contemplation in the midst of love. He speaks of how he learned from his grandmother how to love the Virgin. But there at the Basilica of Guadalupe, it was so clear: Mary's house, the dwelling place of God in the flesh, the assembly of those related to him because he chose to be related to her. He speaks of her here, present to him and present to us: "Let us look at the Blessed Mother from within our own sufferings, our own fear, hopelessness, sadness, and say to her, 'What can I offer since I am not learned?' We look to our Mother with eyes that express our thoughts" (homily, February 13, 2016).

And so it is that the Holy Father shows us a way of prayer that is transparent and translucent to the provocative appearance of the Word made flesh. The narrative of the Gospel is the Lord's plea to us to drink deeply of his compassion. Whether at Mass or in our rooms with the doors closed, the vista of the Lord is what we are offered if only we take the first step and respond to him by saying, "Lord, I want to see." And he draws us into the mystery of his crucified flesh, raised in glory and even now drawing his people into his very own gaze, transforming us into agents of his grace.

Bishop Daniel E. Flores was appointed bishop of Brownsville, Texas, in 2009. He tweets at Amigo de Frodo—@bpdflores—and his blog, "En Pocas Palabras," can be found at bishopflores.blogspot.com.

Reform

Cardinal Óscar Rodríguez Maradiaga, SDB

In the dictionary of the Royal Spanish Academy, the word *reforma* has various meanings. One of them is: the action and effect of reforming or reforming one's self; or what is proposed, projected, or executed as an innovation or improvement of something. And with all due respect to that concept, Pope Francis's reform is something else.

In Sacred Scripture, both the Old and New Testaments, the references to the biblical-theological concept of reform are innumerable. It is enough here to emphasize only one: the reform of our Lord Jesus Christ who "passed through this world doing good and fulfilling the will of His Father." One of the greatest and most fundamental reforms that our Lord Jesus faced concerned the concept or image of God that existed during his earthly lifetime. He took on the task of placing the authentic and true image of God on the religious table of his world and for generations to come: as Psalm 103 says: "Merciful and gracious is the LORD, slow to anger, abounding in mercy" (v. 8). The great reform of Jesus Christ was in being the image and likeness of His Father. For some, it was reform; for others, change; for still others, annoyance; and for some, revolution.

And it is here that we connect with Pope Francis's concept of reform. To do this, we must go back to his days as cardinal archbishop of Buenos Aires. There are many sources, however in this case, only one is clear: his 2007 book, *True Power Is Service*. Not all publishing houses were convinced of the importance of publishing his books. Those who did were not mistaken. In the book in question, there is a compilation of speeches, conferences, and homilies addressed to priests, laypeople, married couples: in short, everyone. Some were a call not just for a reform of mentality, but for pastoral conversion—calls that were sometimes described as being revolutionary. They were calls for an authentic reform of vocations, of commitment, of a life of faith, of witness that did not violate nor change the doctrine of the church's magisterium but rather placed our Lord Jesus at the centre of everything and everyone.

When Pope Benedict XVI resigned and the world's cardinals gathered for pre-conclave meetings in early March 2013, there were a great number of proposals that focused on the next steps awaiting the church with the election of a new Supreme Pontiff. Among them was the need to update the Roman Curia to streamline many processes that seemed very slow. Many cardinals saw the Curia as an organization that was too large, and there was the added difficulty that the pope could not meet with his "council of ministers" with the necessary frequency. Thus arose the proposal of a Council of Cardinals from the five continents, from the "base," that could provide the pope with the information which, for various reasons, did not always reach its final destination.

The Council of Cardinals was announced on April 13, 2013—known as the C8 and, as of July 1, 2014, as the C9 with the inclusion of the Vatican's Secretary of State—mainly to advise the pope on the governance of the universal church and on other related matters; it also had the specific mission of proposing a revision of the apostolic constitution *Pastor Bonus*, which had regulated the Roman Curia since the pontificate of St. John Paul II. At first, many thought it would be a relatively quick process (at maximum taking two years). Certainly, replacing one constitution with a new one did not seem too complicated. But bit by bit, we understood that it wasn't something external but rather a true *reform*.

Let us allow Pope Francis to define his concept:

> There can be no doubt that, for the Curia, the word reform is to be understood in two ways. First of all, it should make the Curia *con-form* to the Good News which must be proclaimed joyously and courageously to all, especially to the poor, the least and the outcast. To make it *con-form* to the signs of our time and to all its human achievements, so as better to meet the needs of the men and women whom we are called to serve. At the same time, this

means *con-forming* the Curia ever more fully to its purpose, which is that of cooperating in the ministry of the Successor of Peter. . . . Consequently, the reform of the Roman Curia must be guided by ecclesiology and directed *in bonum et in servitium* as is the service of the Bishop of Rome. . . . Since the Curia is not an immobile bureaucratic apparatus, reform is first and foremost a sign of life, of a church that advances on her pilgrim way, of a church that is living and for this reason *semper reformanda*, in need of reform because she is alive (speech to Roman Curia, December 22, 2016).

Thus, reform is a process, a path of growth and conversion. The pope, in the same speech to the Curia, said it candidly: "The reform does not have an aesthetical aim to make the Curia more beautiful; it cannot be understood as a sort of face-lift or applying makeup to beautify the elderly curial body, nor plastic surgery to remove wrinkles. Dear brothers and sisters, it isn't wrinkles we need to worry about in the church, but stains!"

In November 2016, the secretary of the Council of Cardinals, Bishop Marcelo Semeraro, was asked by Spanish Catholic magazine *Vida Nueva*: "When you start to reform your house, sometimes you feel that it's better to throw everything away and rebuild it again. Has there not been such a temptation in the Curia?" Certainly not. The pope does not intend to put everything up for discussion and start from scratch. The main question is how the Curia can be improved to respond to the needs of new times. It is not about destroying an instrument of service.

A structure or a people? The pope is very clear on these criteria: in his perspective, it should be noted that the reform will be effective only if is it done with "renewed" men and women and not simply with "new" men and women. It isn't enough to change personnel but members of the Curia must renew themselves spiritually, personally, and professionally. The reform of the Curia is in no way focused on substituting personnel—though without a doubt some of that happens and will happen—but on the conversion of people. In reality, a "continuing formation" will not suffice; "a continuing conversion and purification" is needed above all: "without a change of mentality, efforts at practical improvement will be in vain" (speech to Roman Curia, December 22, 2016).

What has been done? In his 2016 address to the Curia, the pope listed nineteen reforms already carried out. These are:

1. the creation of the Council of Cardinals on April 13, 2013;

2. the institution of the Pontifical Commission for Reference on the Institute for the Works of Religion on June 24, 2013, in order to achieve complete transparency in the activity of what is commonly known as the Vatican Bank;

3. defining the jurisdiction of the judicial authorities of the Vatican City State in criminal matters on July 11, 2013;

4. the institution of the Pontifical Commission for Reference on the Organization of the Economic-Administrative Structure (COSEA) on July 18, 2013, which has been given the task of research, analysis and gathering of information for the study of the organizational and economic problems of the Holy See;

5. the establishment of the Holy See's Financial Security Committee on August 8, 2013, for the prevention and countering of money-laundering, the financing of terrorism and the proliferation of weapons of mass destruction;

6. the consolidation of the Vatican's Financial Intelligence Authority (AIF) on November 15, 2013, for the prevention and countering of illegal activities in the area of monetary and financial dealings;

7. the institution of the Secretariat for the Economy and the Council for the Economy on February 24, 2014, which are tasked with harmonizing the policies of control regarding economic management of the Holy See and Vatican City;

8. the creation of the Office of General Auditor on February 24, 2014, a new agency charged with auditing the dicasteries of the Roman Curia, the institutions connected to the Holy See or associated with it, and the administration of the Governorate of Vatican City.

9. the establishment of the Pontifical Commission for the Protection of Minors on March 22, 2014, in order "to promote the protection of the dignity of minors and vulnerable adults";

10. the transfer of the Ordinary Section of the Administration of the Patrimony of the Apostolic See (APSA) to the Secretariat for the Economy on July 8, 2014;

11. the approval of the statutes of the new economic agencies on February 22, 2015;

12. the institution of the Secretariat for Communication on June 27, 2015, "to respond to the current context of communication" by restructuring the Vatican's various media entities;

13. the reform of the canonical process in cases of declaration of marital nullity on August 15, 2015;

14. the establishment of new law via papal *motu proprio* to prevent negligence on the part of bishops in the exercise of their office on June 4, 2016;

15. the definition of the respective areas of competence of the Secretariat of the Economy and of the Administration of the Patrimony of the Apostolic See (APSA) on July 4, 2016;

16. the institution of the new Dicastery for Laity, Family and Life on August 15, 2016;

17. the institution of the new Dicastery for Promoting Integral Human Development on August 17, 2016;

18. the approval of the statutes of the Secretariat for Communication on September 6, 2016; and,

19. the approval of the Statutes of the Pontifical Academy for Life on October 18, 2016.

With respect to the timeframe given by Pope Francis to complete the reform of the church, it should be noted that the pope does not focus on this aspect because he knows it doesn't depend on him but on God. Bishop Marcelo Semeraro, secretary of the Council of Cardinals, has noted that Pope John XXIII began an extraordinary process, but died before it was completed. Yet, the process—the Second Vatican Council—continued. Time is a factor that makes us codependent to it, and, depending on the attitude with which things are done, we don't see time as a threat but as a favourable resource of processes that continue at a good pace until the path is complete. We have an urgency to finish this process, yes, but the importance of things per se is one thing, and rushing and hastening is another. God gives us time.

From the moment Francis took the initiative to bring about this reform, time began to run and, as it progresses, it will expire as with all human dynamism: as life, youth, and seasons. But in this moment, the progression of the reform is going at a good pace.

Cardinal Óscar Rodríguez Maradiaga is the archbishop of Tegucigalpa, Honduras, and is the coordinator of the Council of Cardinals. He is a member of the Salesians of Don Bosco and has also served as the president of the Honduran bishops' conference and of Caritas Internationalis.

R

Refugee

Rhonda Miska

"We have lost a sense of brotherly sensibility and forgotten how to cry," said Pope Francis during his first papal trip outside of Rome to Lampedusa, a small Mediterranean island that for many is Europe's perilous entry point. This call to solidarity and lament is one of countless challenges Francis has offered on behalf of migrants and refugees whom he calls "brothers and sisters to be welcomed, respected and loved."

Pope Francis threw a wreath of flowers in the water at Lampedusa, spoke of his grief as "a painful thorn" in his heart, recalled the story of the Good Samaritan, and lamented "globalized indifference." The "penitential liturgy" there was a public expression of his commitment to the peripheries, especially to the estimated 65 million men, women, and children worldwide forcibly displaced from their homes. Francis also offered greetings to "those Muslim immigrants who this evening begin the fast of Ramadan," making clear his concern for all—not just Catholics—from the beginning of his papacy.

At Lampedusa, Francis called for a "concrete change of heart"—a call echoed in his homilies, writings, interviews, and actions. In April 2016, he travelled to the Moria refugee camp in Lesbos, Greece, a locked facility surrounded by razor wire, telling the Syrian refugees interned there, "I simply want to be with you and hear your stories." And he brought twelve Syrian Muslim refugees back to Rome with him. That same year, Francis washed the feet of Catholic, Coptic Christian, Muslim, and Hindu asylum-seekers in Castelnuovo di Porto outside Rome during Holy Week.

These prophetic actions of accompaniment and hospitality were done against a backdrop of increased xenophobia in Europe after terror attacks in Brussels and Paris. Moreover, these public works of mercy happened in the context of the Extraordinary Jubilee Year of Mercy.

Pope Francis's compelling actions of welcome, compassion, and service to refugees are undergirded by clear statements about the environmental, economic, and political/military root causes that push people from their homes.

The pope starkly denounces the root causes and social evils that displace people. In *Laudato Si'* (25), he recognizes that though people forced to flee because of environmental degradation are "not recognized by international conventions as refugees, they bear the loss of the lives they have left behind, without enjoying any legal protection whatsoever." While displaced people might be classified as "refugees," "unaccompanied alien children," "undocumented immigrants," "asylum seekers," or "internally displaced people" and thus treated differently in their respective contexts, for Pope Francis, they are all worthy of respect and integration.

In addition to recognizing "climate refugees," Francis also names the role of economic factors in displacing people. In *Evangelii Gaudium* he decries the "idolatry of money and the dictatorship of an impersonal economy lacking a truly human response" and calls for a church that is "poor and with the poor."

Moreover, Pope Francis has decried armed conflicts that displace people. At a 2016 conference for Jesuit alumni, Francis spoke of refugees' "inalienable right to live in peace and to aspire to a better future for their sons and daughters." In November 2015, he visited the Central African Republic—where a two-year sectarian war has forced many from their homes—and called on combatants to "put down [their] weapons of death." On July 5, 2016, Francis proclaimed that "peace in Syria is possible," and called for a political, not military, solution to the nation's bloody civil war—one of his many denunciations of the violence that had forced 5.5 million Syrians to flee.

Pope Francis also has articulated this Gospel-centred vision of human dignity and the common good in specific European and North American contexts. In March 2017, after the United Kingdom voted to leave the European Union, at a meeting with twenty-seven European national leaders, Francis called for a "spirit of solidarity and subsidiarity" in the European Union and for rejection of "false forms of security" that would close doors. During a February 17, 2016, flight from Mexico to Rome, amid a US presidential campaign marked by anti-Mexican rhetoric and talk of a border wall, the pope said, "A person who thinks only of building walls, wherever it may be, and not of building bridges, is not Christian. This is not in the Gospel."

But Pope Francis goes far beyond challenging the affluent to see refugees as objects of charity by calling on people to see refugees as agents of evangelization and missionary disciples with much to teach (EG 198). "Each one of you refugees who knock on our doors has the face of God and is the body of Christ," he told refugees at the Jesuit Refugee Service-run Astalli Centre in Rome in September 2013. "Treated as a burden, a problem, a cost, instead you are a gift." He also emphasized the gifts refugees bring as peacemakers, stating that refugees "know the roads that lead to peace because they know the acrid odour of war."

While the dominant rhetoric in many nations portrays displaced people as "problems to be solved," for Pope Francis, they are at the centre, not the margins, of community. As he said in his message for the 2014 World Day for Migrants and Refugees, "Jesus, Mary and Joseph knew what it meant to leave their own country. . . . They were forced to take flight and seek refuge in Egypt." In their sojourning, refugees mirror the church who "herself is a missionary disciple" (EG 40). In his January 19, 2014, Angelus message, Francis spoke directly to migrants: "Dear friends, you are close to the church's heart, because the church is a people on a journey towards the kingdom of God."

Evangelii Gaudium presents the paradoxical truth that the church exists to evangelize and simultaneously needs to be evangelized by those on the peripheries. The poor, particularly displaced people who mirror the Holy Family's displacement, are a living symbol of the church as God's pilgrim people.

Pope Francis's call to see migrants and refugees as agents of evangelization resonates deeply with my experience. My own Catholic faith and trust in God have been touched in powerful, humbling ways through the accompaniment of immigrants, refugees, and asylum-seekers. In 2014, I served as a legal assistant to unaccompanied children from Central America fleeing violence and seeking to reunite with family in the United States. After taking the testimony of a fifteen-year-old boy about leaving Honduras and journeying north, and confirming he knew about his upcoming court appearance, I asked if he had any questions.

"When I go to court, will Jesus be with me?" he asked, after a thoughtful pause.

I was speechless momentarily before responding, "Yes, Jesus will be with you." For those of us from backgrounds of privilege and security, such encounters prophetically stretch our own confession of reliance on God's providence and call us to deeper personal and collective conversion.

When I read Francis's encouragement to those accompanying refugees at the Astalli Centre to "always witness to the beauty of this encounter," I recalled another heart-stretching encounter with a different asylum-seeking Central American boy. During the interview, after he described the gang violence that claimed his brother's life, I asked this boy why he came to the United States. His answer took my breath away: *Porque yo tengo dignidad humana y quiero vivir en paz*—"Because I have human dignity and I want to live in peace." While this boy had lost his home and his family, he retained hope, purpose, and a sense of God-given identity.

Shortly before Christmas 2016, after interpreting a legal consultation between my attorney colleague and an asylum-seeking Guatemalan teenaged girl, she thanked us, saying: *Dios está con ustedes*—"God is with you." In listening to the voices of our refugee brothers and sisters, we can hear God's name spoken and be evangelized anew.

Rhonda Miska is a novice with the Sinsinawa Dominican Sisters in Sinsinawa, Wisconsin. She holds an MA from the Boston College School of Theology and Ministry and served as a Jesuit Volunteer in Nicaragua. She has ministered with immigrants, refugees, and asylum-seekers in different contexts for over a decade. She dedicates this chapter to her colleague, immigration attorney Yer Vang, with respect and admiration.

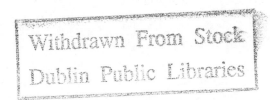

Saint Francis

Michael Perry, OFM

It is no exaggeration to say that for Cardinal Jorge Bergoglio to choose the name of St. Francis of Assisi as his patron as pope he was sending a message to the church and the world about values that would guide his reflections and actions. In homilies, speeches, letters, exhortations, and encyclicals, Pope Francis has globalized the vision of the saint from Assisi while highlighting what I would identify as six pathways for the church in the world today.

Path of the Poor

On October 13, 2014, Pope Francis spoke in the room where eight hundred years earlier, Francis of Assisi had renounced his "life in the world"—abandoning all for the sake of the poor Christ. The pope emphasized movement, going outward towards all people, following the pathway that leads to encounter and companionship with those who are poor. "We are called to be poor . . . learning how to be with the poor, to share with those who lack basic necessities, to touch the flesh of Christ," he said. The pope placed before the world's eyes images that coalesce into the love affair of the *poverello*—stories of personal encounters and sufferings that move hearts and shape human attitudes. Like Francis of Assisi, the pope embraced those who were sick and disabled. In the public square outside of the Basilica of St. Mary of the Angels, he created a space for dialogue with young people of Umbria who came in search of mercy and pardon. He called out to bishops, priests, religious, and pastoral workers to take the Gospel pathway that leads to the margins, to embrace and help beggars, and to welcome migrants searching for a place where they might experience compassion, freedom, peace, and hope.

Path of Jesus

The foundational Gospel images present in the life and writings of St. Francis of Assisi have come to the fore in the actions and words of Pope Francis: Jesus "became poor . . . so that by his poverty you might become rich" (2 Cor 8.9); Jesus "born naked, placed in a manger, dying naked and crucified"; and Jesus on a cross, not dead but alive! It was at the small Church of San Damiano—where Francis of Assisi received his calling to follow the crucified and resurrected Jesus—that Pope Francis began his Assisi pilgrimage in 2013. In a moment of foolish Franciscan exuberance, I reminded Pope Francis of five words Jesus communicated to the Saint of Assisi: "Go, and repair my church." These words serve as metaphor for how the saint embraced and loved the world and all of its inhabitants. Pope Francis has embraced this message and made it his own in word and deed. For both the Saint of Assisi and the Jesuit pope, the call is not to create some sociological or politically ideological response to a problem. Rather, both have made the choice to follow in the footprints of Jesus, "to imitate him, to follow him to the end" (speeches in Assisi, October 4, 2013).

Path of an Affective Spiritual Tradition

It is significant that Francis is the first pope since Gregory XVI (1831–46) thoroughly steeped in a distinctive evangelical tradition of spirituality. His is a charismatic inheritance that has now become "ecclesially" global. It is an important element in his evangelizing methodology and call for pastoral discernment. In this way, the pope shares with Ignatius of Loyola and Francis of Assisi a deeply grounded evangelical spirituality of conversion and mission. This path always begins with a heartfelt response to the initiative of God's love taking flesh in the incarnation, coming to fullness in the gaze of love, and in the life poured out for us, inviting humans to participate in the life of the Spirit. Francis of Assisi welcomed the call to join with God who humbled himself, taking on human likeness, embracing human brokenness, reminding humanity of its innate goodness and holiness. It is through the embrace of those who are broken that Francis of Assisi and Pope Francis demonstrate the full implications of the incarnation—God dwelling in our midst, validating our dignity as beloved children. For Pope Francis, the embrace of brothers and sisters living with disabilities or other infirmities serves as the public embodiment of the Ignatian "composition of place," the humble recognition that "God dwells in creatures," especially the poor. Franciscan and Ignatian spirituality meet in the loving embrace of those who are poor and excluded.

Pope Francis's fascination with St. Francis did not begin on the day of his election as the successor of St. Peter when the former archbishop of São Paulo, Brazil, Cardinal Claudio Hummes, OFM, whispered the now famous words "Do not forget the poor!" into Jorge Bergoglio's ear. His novitiate bookshelf revealed his fascination with the life of St. Francis (Austen Ivereigh, *The Great Reformer: Francis and the Making of a Radical Pope*, p. 67). The cardinal of Buenos Aires also was well aware of the impact of Franciscan spiritual writer García de Cisneros's *Book of Exercises for the Spiritual Life* on Ignatius, especially the focus on the affective encounter with the Word of God, or feeling the Word present within one's entire being. Saint Augustine spoke of the transformative power of this type of interior prayer in his *Confessions* (10.6). Francis of Assisi tapped into this tradition in his *Office of the Passion*, and reenacted it in the public square in Greccio. While St. Bonaventure codified this method in the *Journey of the Mind into God* (chs. 4, 7), Ignatius systematized it in his *Spiritual Exercises*.

It is this affective approach to spirituality, grounded in authentic encounter with the living Lord of Life, that has influenced Pope Francis's thinking about St. Francis, especially where he writes about the transformation of the interior affections of the heart: "The true battlefield where violence and peace meet is the human heart" (Mark 7:21; homily, March 19, 2013). In Assisi, Pope Francis reminded the young that they are to go forward with the "Gospel in heart and hands" (October 4, 2013). Here the incarnational experience of St. Francis and St. Ignatius meet, giving birth to a spirituality of discernment that leads people on a transformative journey, and the embodiment of the Gospel in word and deed. The last chapter of *Evangelii Gaudium* on "Spirit-filled Evangelizers" finds its depths in this long spiritual inheritance. The Word dwells in the heart and takes flesh through the body. The fruits of this transformational journey are peace, joy, love, mercy, reconciliation, encounter, accompaniment, justice, compassion, and respect for creation (Message for World Day of Peace, January 1, 2017). These virtues are reflected in the spiritual imagination and practices of both saints, Francis and Ignatius.

Path of Living Example

While many of the pope's reflections on Francis of Assisi have been personal and local, he has also taken the saint as "the inspirational ideal of my pontificate" (Letter to Bishop of Assisi, April 16, 2017). In a popular world driven not by words but by images, the message surfaces most effectively in the media coverage of some of his most significant gestures, bodily public performances of the Gospel way of life. Washing the feet of men and women, believers and unbelievers, on Holy Thursday (March 2013); visiting prisoners; travelling to the island of Lampedusa to identify with the suffering (July 2013); inviting homeless men to share his breakfast on his first birthday as pope—all are gestures related to human dignity, stories reminiscent of the universal fraternal gestures that marked the life of Francis of Assisi. The picture went viral when the pope "hugged and kissed" Vincio Riva, a tumorous man repulsive to the eyes but like the leper in Assisi, an icon of the living Christ (November 2013). People who gathered at the Festival of Forgiveness held at St. Peter's Basilica in Rome (March 28–29, 2014), witnessed the pontiff kneeling down in public, asking for the forgiveness of his sins. Eight hundred years previously townsfolk gathered in Assisi witnessed the young Francis of Assisi doing public penance for his sins. In May 2014, while in the Holy Land, the pope kissed the hands of Holocaust survivors and included Jews and Muslims in his official travelling party, gestures pointing to an encounter nearly eight hundred years earlier between Francis of Assisi and Al Malik Al Kamal, Sultan and military leader during the Fifth Crusade. In September 2015, at the canonization of the Franciscan missionary Fr. Junípero Serra, the pope met privately with representatives of the Native American community to pursue the path of forgiveness and reconciliation. A line of the *Canticle of Creatures* had been acted out with the indigenous protectors of the land: "Blessed are those who endure in peace, for by You, Most High, shall they be crowned." On August 5, 2016, to highlight the year of mercy, Pope Francis made a personal pilgrimage to the Shrine of the Portiuncula in Assisi, linking the pardon sought by Francis of Assisi for the people of his times with the pope's desire to promote mercy and peace in his. In an April 16, 2017, letter to the Bishop of Assisi, the pope wrote: "The Christian is not one who speaks about the poor, no! He is one who encounters them, who looks them in the eye, who touches them." For both Francis and Francis, Christian discipleship is deeply interpersonal; it is "in your face" and filled with grace.

Path of the Teaching Word

Redolent with basic evangelical themes of the Franciscan and Ignatian tradition (e.g., centrality of conversion to Jesus Christ and the poor, practices of mercy, contemplative seeing, fraternity, the role of the Holy Spirit, and discernment), *Evangelii Gaudium* makes no overt references to Francis of Assisi. *Lumen Fidei* links the example of Francis with that of Mother Teresa, thus bridging the thirteenth with the twenty-first century: "To those who suffer, God does not provide arguments which explain everything; rather, his response is that of an accompanying presence. . . . In Christ, God himself wishes to share this path with us" (LF 57). In contrast, *Laudato Si'* reflects deeply on Francis of Assisi's *Canticle of Creatures* as particularly pertinent to the contemporary world. Here St. Francis becomes "the example par excellence of care for the vulnerable and of an integral ecology lived out joyfully and authentically." The *poverello* "shows us just how inseparable the bond is between concern for nature, justice for the poor, commitment to society, and interior peace" (LS 10). *Laudato Si'* challenges the contemporary world to move beyond the "economic calculus" prevalent in the languages of mathematics and biology towards a fraternal affection that manifests "care for all that exists" (LS 11). Nature itself is "a magnificent book in which God speaks to us and grants us a glimpse of his infinite beauty and goodness" (LS 12). In *Amoris Laetitia*, the pope meditates on the "mystery of Christmas and the secret of Nazareth," a direct reference to the spirituality of the incarnation in the life of Francis of Assisi. Francis of Assisi's fascination with the "incarnation of the Word in a human family" captures both the path now opening for the church and a path that can fill "Christian families with hope and joy" (AL 65).

Path of Reform through Mission to World

The Gospel paths that Pope Francis links with Francis of Assisi are placed throughout his writings in the context of a church and world in desperate need of reform. The centrality of the poor; conversion to the incarnate, crucified, and risen Christ; the reclaiming of a spiritual inheritance; teaching by example and word—all of these push believer and unbeliever alike to move out of themselves into the city streets and rural outposts in quest of a more profound humanization of society.

Convergence of Six Pathways

Interpreted in their appropriate context, these pathways present an "integral ecology" of a prophetic missionary Gospel. Francis of Assisi's direct encounter and accompaniment of the poor—his personalization of those who are suffering—stands over against "the laws of competition and the survival of the fittest," the "globalization of indifference," characteristic of contemporary economic systems (EG 52–56). Embedded in the concrete actions of "dialogue" and fraternal solidarity with those who are suffering is a new civic vision calling for inclusion, the redistribution of goods, and promotion and defence of universal human dignity (LS 106–36). The embodiment of a discipleship of mercy and joy in God and neighbour provides a healing balm in a society that traps our desire for the infinite in an endless cycle of consumption and violence. Appreciating the world as God's creation that belongs to all creatures as brothers and sisters speaks a prophetic fraternal word in a world too often depreciating people through a "globalization of the technocratic paradigm." Lastly, learning to contemplate—to see through prayer with compassionate and open eyes the suffering world in all its circumstances in the same way that God sees the world—will engender in the believer a commitment to this "common home" filled with beauty, actions of peace, demonstrations of joy, and works of justice (Message for World Day of Peace, January 1, 2017).

In choosing Francis of Assisi as the "inspirational ideal of his pontificate" Pope Francis, a man radically rooted in an Ignatian spirituality, has revealed on a global scale the riches embedded in the spiritual vision of two great saints. In setting this spiritual practice and path as a counter image and voice to some of our contemporary ills, he has re-established the link between this world and the next, between body and spirit, between spirituality, doctrine, and practice. For Franciscans, he has illuminated in a new way the roots of our evangelical charism and challenged us to a missionary discipleship in the footsteps of Jesus, Mary, and Francis and

Clare of Assisi, thus revealing the true path towards recovering the joy of the Gospel.

Fr. Michael Perry is the 120th successor of St. Francis of Assisi as the minister general of the Franciscan Order of Friars Minor. Fr. Joe Chinnici, OFM, provided invaluable assistance in preparing this article.

Satan

Gregory K. Hillis

On Pentecost Sunday in 2013, two months after his election as pontiff, Pope Francis performed an exorcism in St. Peter's Square. That was the rumour that surfaced after a YouTube video of the pope praying over a young man in a wheelchair appeared online. In the video, the pope places both his hands on the man and prays. Almost immediately, the man's mouth opens wide and he reportedly roars like a lion. Pope Francis continues praying for a few seconds before getting whisked away by concerned security guards.

For the record, the pope's spokesperson at the time, Jesuit Fr. Federico Lombardi, denied that this was an exorcism. However, the fact that this video led to such speculation came as no surprise given how frequently Pope Francis mentioned the devil in his first two months in office, both in his public addresses and homilies as well as in the morning reflections he gave in the chapel of Santa Marta. Since those early months, the pope's references to Satan have continued unabated. Indeed, a search on the Vatican website reveals that so far during his tenure, Pope Francis has mentioned the devil as often as Pope St. John Paul II and Pope Benedict XVI combined.

Francis's focus on the devil is due in no small part to his Jesuit background. In a speech to the community of Jesuit writers at *La Civiltà Cattolica* three months after his election, Pope Francis argued that Jesuits are specialists in discerning what comes from God and what comes from the devil. Our first Jesuit pope appears to take such discernment seriously, although he is aware that some may find his focus on Satan incongruous in the modern world. He knows there are some who deny the reality of the devil, but he is clear that Satan is real, and is someone we must constantly fight. "Look out, the devil exists!" he declared in an April 2014 homily at Santa Marta: "The devil exists in the twenty-first century. We mustn't be naïve. We must learn from the Gospel how to fight against him." In another homily from the same year, he declared that the devil is not "a myth, a figure, an idea, the idea of evil." Satan "exists and we have to fight against him," he said.

Where is it that Pope Francis discerns Satan working today? While he pins responsibility on the devil for fostering hatred and persecution against Christians as well as fomenting war between nations, Francis focuses most of his attention on the way Satan cultivates divisiveness in the church. Pope Francis is emphatic that the devil's principal job is to divide. The devil/Satan loves division and works continually to provoke discord.

According to Pope Francis, the devil provokes disunity at all levels of the church, local and universal, within particular communities and between members of the church throughout the world, from cardinals and bishops to parishioners in the pews. In a speech to members of the charismatic movement, Pope Francis warned that the devil hates the family; that he strives to foster hatred and disunity among family members. To a group of cloistered nuns, he warned that the devil will stop at nothing to disrupt the monastic community through gossip and competition. And Francis told the clergy in Caserta, Italy, that the devil strives to foster disunity within dioceses, and between priests and their bishop. In clerical relationships, instead of joy, the devil uses the weapon of gossip, which leads to resentment, anger, and hatred.

In a January 2014 homily at Santa Marta, Francis contrasted the disunity that so often characterizes the church today with the idealized portrayal of the early Christian community in Acts 4:31-37. This passage provides for us an icon of what the church was, and how it can and should be: a church of "harmony and peace." Unfortunately, the church's unity didn't last. Humility and love gave way to power struggles and infighting. Peace gave way to battles rooted in envy and gossip. Instead of love and forgiveness, hatred and enmity prevailed. And all of this was due to the "father of division," the devil. Whereas Christ through his Spirit endeavours to unify through humility and love, the devil seeks to divide through pride and hatred, both of which manifest themselves in gossip, envy, and infighting.

We see this happen in the case of the Corinthians, as Pope Francis noted in a September 2016 homily at Santa Marta on 1 Corinthians 11:17–26. Here we see a case of the devil attacking the very heart of Christian unity, the Eucharist. The pope argues that the devil, knowing that unity rooted in love characterizes the church, seeks to destroy the church through division. For the devil knows that "divisions in the church do not allow the kingdom of God to grow; they do not allow the Lord to be seen clearly, as he is." The devil thus sows "theological and ideological divisions" that threaten to tear apart the one body of Christ. He does this by fostering jealousy and greed, and particularly through the "terrorism of gossip."

How do we as Christians fight against the divisiveness fostered by Satan? According to Pope Francis, the answer is found through dialogue. Throughout his papacy thus far, Francis has emphasized the preeminence of dialogue, urging Catholics, as he does in *Evangelii Gaudium*, to walk "the path of dialogue." Given how frequently he refers to Satan's divisive work in the church, it is no accident that Francis also reiterates the unifying nature of dialogue rooted in love. Whereas jealousy, envy, and gossip are the fruit of the devil and create rifts between believers, humility, meekness, and becoming all things to all are the principles of dialogue rooted in the love of Christ, a point the pope made in two homilies preached on subsequent days at Santa Marta in January 2014.

In the first homily, Francis used the story of Saul's jealousy of David (1 Sam 18–19) as a launching pad to discuss the way in which the devil tears apart Christian community. Francis noted that Saul had just secured a great victory, but that anger gripped him when he heard others praise David. Envy and jealousy are, according to the pope, the gates through which the devil enters the world, and it is by means of them that he creates rifts between believers. Through envy and jealousy, bitterness comes to characterize the community. Worse still is that gossip, which is "the devil's weapon," becomes rampant. "Gossip divides communities," the pope stated, "it destroys communities."

In his homily the following day, the pope contrasted the humility of dialogue with the envy and jealousy he discussed the day before. Given the chance to kill Saul (1 Sam 24), David instead "chose the path of dialogue to make peace." Such dialogue is difficult, particularly when it involves dialogue with those who hate. But it is only "with dialogue that we build bridges of peace in relationships rather than walls that distance us." To dialogue is to embrace humility and love above envy and jealousy, to see the image of God in the other person, and thus to reject the prideful hatred of Satan. To dialogue is to follow the humble path of Jesus, and it is through such dialogue that the church can attain the unity that rejects Satanic divisiveness.

Pope Francis's portrayal of Satan's divisiveness helps us understand more thoroughly why he argues that dialogue must characterize the church. A church that is dominated by infighting and gossip is a church that has fallen prey to Satan's influence, for such disunity can only be rooted in pride that is closed to love. A dialogical church, however, is one that rejects Satan in favour of genuine love for the other, including— as was the case with David and Saul—love for those who do not love us. We would do well, as we continue to discuss and debate theological and moral issues, to pay heed to Pope Francis's vision.

Gregory K. Hillis is an associate professor of theology at Bellarmine University in Louisville, Kentucky. He has published on patristic theology, ecumenism, Pope Francis, and Thomas Merton. He is currently working on a book on Thomas Merton.

Second Vatican Council

Archbishop Diarmuid Martin

When Fr. Antonio Spadaro interviewed Pope Francis for *La Civiltà Cattolica* early in his pontificate, one of the questions he posed regarded Vatican II. "What did the Second Vatican Council accomplish?" he asked Pope Francis. "What does it mean?" Spadaro was expecting the pope to give a long and articulate response. The pope's short response seemed to surprise him.

"Vatican II was a re-reading of the Gospel in light of contemporary culture," Francis said. "Vatican II produced a renewal movement that simply comes from the same Gospel. Its fruits are enormous. Just recall the liturgy. The work of liturgical reform has been a service to the people as a re-reading of the Gospel from a concrete historical situation. Yes, there are hermeneutics of continuity and discontinuity, but one thing is clear: the dynamic of reading the Gospel, actualizing its message for today—which was typical of Vatican II—is absolutely irreversible."

Unlike his immediate predecessors, Francis had not attended Vatican II. Yet, his view of the council is unique. Pope Francis embraces Vatican II as a moment in which the church, through a dynamic reading of the Gospel, reached out in a new way. The council and its application are the key to understanding Francis's pontificate and also in many ways his hope for renewal in the church.

Curiously, there is a sense in which if you wish to capture Pope Francis's understanding of the council you will find the best interpretation in the words of Pope John XXIII. Pope John had seen how the church must reach out in dialogue and bring the message of Jesus Christ more incisively into the heart of contemporary culture.

In words that could be those today of Pope Francis, Pope John said at the opening of the council in 1962: "Our duty is not only to guard this precious treasure [the deposit of faith], as if we were concerned only with antiquity, but to dedicate ourselves with an earnest will and without fear to that work which our era demands of us, pursuing thus the path which the Church has followed for twenty centuries."

And he continued: "The substance of the ancient doctrine of the deposit of faith is one thing, and the way in which it is presented is another. And it is the latter that must be taken into great consideration—with patience if necessary—everything being measured in the forms and proportions of a magisterium which is predominantly pastoral in character."

Pope John never denied that there were errors in doctrine within the church and that the clashes with certain elements of modern culture could indeed lead to even great confusion about doctrine. The approach of the council, Pope John proclaimed, should not be one just of condemnation and correction. "Nowadays, however, the spouse of Christ prefers to make use of the medicine of mercy rather than that of severity. She considers that she meets the needs of the present day by demonstrating the validity of her teaching rather than by condemnations," he said, using words that again could be those of Pope Francis today.

The language of the council was the language of openness. Years later at the opening of the Jubilee of Mercy, which started in December 2015 on the fiftieth anniversary of the closing of Vatican II, Pope Francis recalled how the council had opened the church to the world. Francis said: "This anniversary cannot be remembered only for the legacy of the Council's documents, which testify to a great advance in faith. Before all else, the Council was an encounter. A genuine *encounter between the church and the men and women of our time.* An encounter marked by the power of the Spirit, who impelled the church to emerge from the shoals which for years had kept her self-enclosed so as to set out once again, with enthusiasm, on her missionary journey."

For Pope Francis, the postconciliar church today must be missionary and must reach out with the same power and enthusiasm as the council did. "Wherever there are people, the church is called to reach out to them and to bring the joy of the Gospel, and the mercy and forgiveness of God," Francis said at the opening of the holy year. "The Jubilee [of Mercy] challenges us to this openness, and demands that we not neglect *the spirit which emerged from Vatican II, the spirit of the Samaritan*, as Blessed Paul VI expressed it at the conclusion of the Council."

In a video message to a theological conference in Argentina in September 2015, Pope Francis recalled:

> One of the main contributions of the Second Vatican Council was precisely seeking a way to overcome the divorce between theology and pastoral care, between faith and life. I dare say that the Council has revolutionized to some extent the status of theology—the believer's way of doing and thinking. . . . We must take on the work, the arduous work of distinguishing the message of Life from its forms of transmission, from its cultural elements that have a time encoded within. . . . Avoiding this exercise in discernment leads in one way or another to a betrayal of the content of the message. It causes the Good News to cease being new and above all good; it becomes sterile, emptied of all its creative strength, its healing and resurrecting strength. . . . Doctrine is not a closed system, void of the dynamic capacity to pose questions, doubts, inquiries. . . . To guard doctrine requires fidelity to what has been received and—at the same time—it requires taking into account the one speaking, the one receiving, who is known and loved.

Looking back at Pope Francis's response to Spadaro's question, we can see that the pope does not get lost in controversies about the interpretation of Vatican II. He takes up anew the basic inspiration of Pope John in calling the council. Pope Francis recognizes that the challenge of reaching out with the Gospel to contemporary culture remains vital. He takes up the insights of Pope John with renewed vigour and sets out to lead the church day by day, through his words and his example, as Washington, DC, Cardinal Donald Wuerl said recently, "reconnecting the church with the energy of the Second Vatican Council."

Archbishop Diarmuid Martin leads the Archdiocese of Dublin, Ireland. He has previously served as the Holy See's Permanent Observer to the United Nations Office at Geneva and as secretary of the Vatican's former Pontifical Council for Justice and Peace.

Service

Phyllis Zagano

We find the word *diakonia* throughout the gospels. In just about every language of the world—from Afrikaans to Zulu—*diakonia* translates to, or at least signifies, the same word: *diakonia*. That is, people use *diakonia* to mean *diakonia*. It is maddening for a word to define a word, but what is this *diakonia*? What does it mean?

The simplest meaning of *diakonia* is "service," and many translations of many Bible passages give only "service" as its meaning. If *diakonia* is service, then what does service mean? Some say the New Testament only uses it to mean waiting on tables—serving food—or distributing alms. Some say it means management. Some say it means official duty.

No matter which, in gospel passages, this *diakonia*-service is always active, always voluntary, and always Spirit-filled. It is a service of and through the teachings of Christ, cheerfully other-directed, prayerfully considered, and graciously given. Many translations use the word "ministry," especially where *diakonia* appears in the context of faith (Acts 6:1-7; 21:19, 20; Rom 12:3, 7; 1 Cor 16:13, 15; Eph 4:12, 13; 1 Tim 1:12, 14; 2 Tim 4:5, 7). That faith, that *pístis*, is the Lord's inborn persuasion, the movement of the Holy Spirit.

For Pope Francis, service is just that. Service is faith-filled ministry born of the inspiration of the Spirit and to which we are all called.

Who serves, and how? Francis is especially mindful of the service of authority. We each and all participate in authority of one sort or another. We wield it and we cooperate with it. He says, "Authority . . . is meant for the service of the common good" (*Lumen Fidei* 55). And, "our joint service in this world must extend to God's creation" (Joint Catholic–Lutheran statement, October 31, 2016). No matter our stations in life, we are all part of that "joint service." Properly lived, the service that Francis describes creates and recreates us as other Christs in the world.

One of Francis's titles is "Servant of the servants of God." Whether speaking of his own or anyone else's authority, he is clear. The only authentic exercise of authority is through service. He has said: "Let us never forget that authentic power is service, and that the pope too, when exercising power, must enter ever more fully into that service which has its radiant culmination on the Cross. . . . He must open his arms to protect all of God's people and embrace with tender affection the whole of humanity, especially the poorest, the weakest, the least important. . . . Only those who serve with love are able to protect!" (Mass for inauguration of Petrine ministry, March 19, 2013).

So, service must be done "with love"? We often connect service with charitable works, but charity not born of love, not impelled by the Spirit, is only social service. It is good, but it is not the *diakonia*-service to which Francis calls us. For him, service grows and gives evidence to a life of prayer, and only a genuine life of prayer includes genuine service.

The two are inextricably bound. Francis says: "We can no longer separate a religious life, a pious life, from service to brothers and sisters. . . . We can no longer divide prayer, the encounter with God in the sacraments, from listening to the other, closeness to his life, especially to his wounds. Remember this: love is the measure of faith" (Angelus, October 26, 2014).

All things being equal, the person who dismisses another in need to attend to "prayer" is not praying at all. Francis obviously does not mean for us to upend the balance of our lives. We both need and deserve our private time and prayer lives. But if our prayer becomes a shield for self-centredness, we are only entertaining our own egos. We are not really praying.

That certain self-centredness can cause us to avoid genuine service. It can cause us to tend to leave "service" to the professionals and end it there. We may pat a back or write a cheque, but we are distant from others. Francis reminds us that God asks us to get involved, not necessarily as professional ministers, but as simple Christians: "The task the Lord gives us . . . is the vocation to charity in which each of Christ's disciples puts his or her entire life at his service, so to grow each day in love" (Mass for the canonization of Mother Teresa, September 4, 2016).

To put our entire lives at the service of Christ is to put our lives at each other's service with love. We have neighbours, we have friends, we have relatives, we have co-workers. To see each as a member of the body of Christ is both our duty and our vocation.

And these require humility. Not the misplaced humility of those who think they are completely unworthy, that all they can do is live as door-mats for others. It is the graced humility we learn as God's beloved, called in all our dignity to first be who we are and then to do what we can.

With that understanding, with that sort of humility, we can under-stand the pope's words: "Service is the work of the humble, today we have heard it in the Gospel. Jesus came to serve, not to be served. And hope is the virtue of the humble" (address to the Community of Christian Life, April 30, 2015). So, how to do this? How to live humbly and with hope in service to others, and yet maintain our sense of self? And what are the traps? What is the wrong kind of service?

Francis explains:

> There is a kind of "service" which serves others, yet we need to be careful not to be tempted by another kind of service, one which is "self-serving" with regard to others. There is a way to go about serv-ing which is interested in only helping "my people," "our people." This service always leaves "your people" outside, and gives rise to a process of exclusion. All of us are called by virtue of our Christian vocation to that service which truly serves, and to help one another not to be tempted by a "service" which is really "self-serving." All of us are asked, indeed urged, by Jesus to care for one another out of love. Without looking to one side or the other to see what our neighbour is doing or not doing (homily in Havana, Cuba, September 20, 2015).

In essence, when Francis speaks of service he calls us to our baptismal promises; he challenges us to live other-directed Christian lives of prayer and service. He challenges us to be sealed by love. He calls us to be Christ for others, modelling Jesus as we can. As he said early in his papacy: "The life of Jesus is a life for others. It is a life of service" (homily in Rio de Janeiro, Brazil, July 28, 2013).

Phyllis Zagano is senior research associate-in-residence and adjunct professor of religion at Hofstra University in New York and author of many books on spirituality and ministry. A leading expert on women deacons, she was named to the Papal Study Commission on Women in the Diaconate in 2016.

Sheep

Archbishop Justin Welby

I visited Pope Francis in Rome in October 2016 to commemorate and celebrate the fiftieth anniversary of both the historic meeting between our predecessors Archbishop Michael Ramsey and Pope Paul VI and the founding of the Anglican Centre in Rome. Probably the most moving part of that visit was when we came to exchange gifts. I gave the Holy Father a pectoral cross, part of the distinctive insignia of a bishop. This cross was a cross of nails—a symbol of reconciliation that has its origins in the cross made out of nails plucked from the ruins of Coventry Cathedral after it was bombed in the Second World War. Pope Francis gave me a crozier, the head of which was a replica of the crozier of Pope Gregory the Great who sent my predecessor St. Augustine from Rome to Canterbury to spread the Gospel among the English people. The crozier is the basic tool of the shepherd. The actual head of St. Gregory's crozier had been lent to me some months before and had travelled (in its own airplane seat) from Rome to Canterbury to sit among the primates of the Anglican Communion as we met: a visible reminder not only of our connection with the wider church in time and space but also of the pastoral office of the bishop.

The Church of England's rite for the ordination of bishops states: "Bishops are called to serve and care for the flock of Christ. Mindful of the Good Shepherd, who laid down his life for his sheep, they are to love and pray for those committed to their charge, knowing their people and being known by them."

The image of sheep and shepherd is one which has recurred time and again in the teaching and preaching of Pope Francis, right from the early days of his pontificate. In his addresses in his first Holy Week in office in 2013 he coined his memorable phrase exhorting the priests gathered at the Chrism Mass to be shepherds living with "the smell of the sheep." And in that same week at his general audience he spoke at some length about Jesus' parable of the Lost Sheep.

As I reflect on the Holy Father's use of the New Testament's image of sheep and shepherd I am drawn back to two key themes: the pastoral work of the church, its members, and its ministers; and the priority of evangelization.

First, then, the pastoral ministry. In his first general audience (March 27, 2013), the Holy Father expounded the parable of the Lost Sheep and touched on the cost of pastoral ministry and the necessity to seek out the lost, the one who is in need of care. It is easy, he said, to remain in the comfort of the sheepfold, but God calls the Christian to step outside of the sheepfold "in search of the one lost sheep, however far it may have wandered." This is, indeed, what God did in the incarnation—"God stepped outside of himself to come among us" and what Jesus did and continues to do. Consequently it is not possible to stay content within the sheepfold with Jesus, because Jesus has himself stepped outside of the fold. Thus in order to be with him and stay with him, "we have to 'step outside,' to search for the lost sheep together with him."

Pastoral ministry and the model of the Good Shepherd inform the life of all those in ordained ministry in the church. For Pope Francis the pastoral is the priority. There is a need to protect the flock, and to feed the sheep (*Evangelii Gaudium* 171). All of us in ministry find ourselves from time to time asking the question he asked in a homily in Rome on June 6, 2014: "Am I a shepherd or am I just an employee of this NGO called the church?" But to this question the response comes from Jesus in his words to Peter in John 21: "Feed my sheep." "Be shepherds," says Pope Francis, "the rest will come later." And, of course, the pastor knows that he or she is a shepherd first when that pastor serves and relates to the flock so deeply that he or she can be described as living with the "smell of the sheep."

My second reflection is about the task of evangelization, or evangelism and witness. This is one of the priority areas for my own ministry as Archbishop of Canterbury. Later on in that first year of Pope Francis's pontificate he addressed the Ecclesial Convention of the Diocese of Rome and turned on its head the traditional image of the sheepfold, the ninety-nine and the one lost sheep: "Brothers and sisters, we have one sheep. We have lost the other ninety-nine. We must go out, we must go out to them!"

This is the painful reality of the evangelistic task that faces the church, particularly in Europe today. Just as the pastoral ministry of the church requires stepping outside the sheepfold, so does the evangelistic. The secure enclosure of the sheepfold is normally thought of as something comforting that keeps the flock within secure, but the gate of the sheepfold can be left open to let others in as well—and this is not always comfortable. But for Francis and for me it is vital that the church steps outside itself, seeking intentionally to grow and draw others in. But, as the Holy Father said to the Ecclesial Convention in 2013: "It is easier to stay at home, with that one sheep; it is easier with that sheep to comb its fleece, to stroke it . . . but . . . the Lord wants us to be shepherds, he does not want us to fuss with combing fleeces."

The Most Reverend and Right Honourable Justin Welby has been Archbishop of Canterbury since February 2013 and is the leader of the worldwide Anglican Communion.

Sourpuss

James Corkery, SJ

In the Irish neighbourhood where I grew up, there was a group of kids the same age. So we hung out together. We didn't agree on everything, but on one thing we were all clear: Mrs. O. was a "sourpuss." She always berated us. We never saw her smile. She frowned at us and peered suspiciously, sure that whenever she saw us "loitering" (her word) we were "up to no good" (her words also). Even the most charming and funniest of our companions could not cheer her up. Her mind was already made up—the whole of creation was groaning and she was determined to be the lead singer! And clearly she liked the role. If she found any joy at all in life, it was in finding no joy in life! She was very religious too, "a pillar of the church," and disapproving and sharp-tongued about anyone who was not. Her Catholic faith was a very "serious" matter for her, and she bore the burden of it fully—and "burden" it was, as she carried it in her tight-lipped way!—and with just a little ostentation and haughtiness.

Jorge Mario Bergoglio, if he had been a boy with us, would have been allergic to Mrs. O. also (and to Mr. B. and Fr. D. and others of the rather large "sourpuss" brigade that we knew), and he would have been in trouble with his parents for using the word about them—just as we were. I doubt he would have stopped using it, however, mischievous youth that he was (according to one religious sister who taught him), because he has a low tolerance for gloomy, melancholy Christians whose "pickled-pepper faces" contrast with, rather than convey, the joy of the Gospel. Sourpusses are joyless. Instead of living from a profound security in the love of Jesus that assures them of tenderness and forgiveness and that gives them deep-down joy, they live from the pseudo-security of their own uprightness and rectitude. They have no need of mercy because they do everything right, keeping every rule to the letter and following every precept. And not needing mercy themselves, they do not feel the need to offer it to anyone else either—rather, the contrary! They exude vanity, gloom, and self-righteousness. They appear to live the Gospel while missing its merciful centre entirely, unlike the publican in Luke 18:9-14 but dangerously similar to the Pharisee in the same parable.

Sourpusses are inward-looking, self-focused. But the entire thrust of Pope Francis's ministry and of the pastoral care that he wishes people to receive centres on going out. In his apostolic exhortation *Evangelii Gaudium*, his first major document, he sketches the character of the "missionary disciple" who is called to spread the Gospel. Every Christian is meant to be such a disciple, an evangelizer, but Francis knows that this is impossible in the absence of joy; the gloomy do not convince! So he states that "an evangelizer must never look like someone who has just come back from a funeral" (EG 10). At the depths of the Christian evangelizer's life lies a joy that does not evaporate, that cannot be taken away, even amid life's difficulties (EG 6, 10). The true Christian is marked by such joy. Melancholy Christians, with their gloomy, doleful faces, are a contradiction. They have a "pickled-pepper face" (*una faccia da peperoncini all'aceto*), Francis said in his morning Mass homily on May 10, 2013. These are the "sourpusses" who will convince no one because they speak not from joy but from self-preoccupation and self-importance.

"Sourpuss" is not a pleasant word and is surprising on the lips of a pope, even Pope Francis, whose vocabulary is fairly colourful. He uses it to get across something fundamental about being an evangelizer—that one must dare deep trust in God and confidence in God's action in the world. When speaking in *Evangelii Gaudium* about temptations that are faced by pastoral workers, Pope Francis names one of the "more serious" of these as "a defeatism which turns us into querulous and disillusioned pessimists, 'sourpusses'" (EG 85). This defeatism, he says, is characterized by a lack of bold confidence in God's grace and it comes from "an anxious and self-centred lack of trust." The Christian of defeatist attitude, in Francis's view, is ultimately a "sourpuss" who has yielded to a "sterile pessimism" in place of the joy and confidence that rely on God's power made perfect in weakness (see 2 Cor 12:9 and EG 85). "Sourpuss" is an apt term for these defeatists, whose dour, dishwater faces radiate no joy. "Sourpuss" is, of course, the word used in the English translation of *Evangelii Gaudium* but in Spanish, which is Pope Francis's own language, the phrase used is *cara de vinagre*, which means "vinegar-face." The translation of "sourpuss" as used in EG 85 is less vivid or colourful in other languages, for example, in French (*au visage assombri*), in German (*mit düsterem Gesicht*) and in Italian (*dalla faccia scura*). The first means "shadowed" or "darkened," the second, "gloomy" or "sombre," and the third simply "dark." Francis is getting at something more than these adjectives in his use of the term. For him, the "sourpuss" is acidic, biting, driving hope out of people rather than putting joy into them. Sourpusses "annoy" Francis more than just about any other kind of person because they end up substituting the works of adhering meticulously to precepts and practising casuistry over the faith from which flow joy, magnanimity, and largesse. They rely on themselves, and there are many in the church, among our very selves.

Going out, being a people, a *chiesa in uscita*, this is the passion of Francis. And joy goes out. The joy that contrasts with the "sourpuss's" sterile pessimism is a specifically Christian joy that spills beyond those who receive it to go out to the whole world, proclaiming the Good News to all. It is deeper than what is normally referred to as "happiness"; it is more than cheerfulness or having a sunny personality. It is a divine gift that is received not selfishly for oneself but to share, to give away; it is ultimately "missionary" in character. The disciples returning to Jerusalem after the ascension (Luke 24:50-53) are "full of joy." Those sent out two by two, doing great things in the name of Jesus, come back full of amazement at what they have been able to do. The Gospel gives wings to the feet, not gloom to the face. The sourpuss can be transformed, "blown open," by it, Mrs. O. included. She—and the Mrs. O. in each of us!—can be "cured" and transformed by the Gospel. All we have to do is let ourselves be flooded by the joy that wells up from deep within it—*gaudium evangelii*.

Fr. Jim Corkery is an Irish Jesuit priest who teaches systematic theology at the Pontifical Gregorian University in Rome. He is the author of Joseph Ratzinger's Theological Ideas: Wise Cautions and Legitimate Hopes *and co-editor, with Thomas Worcester, SJ, of* The Papacy since 1500: From Italian Prince to Universal Pastor. *He is an associate editor of* The Cambridge Encyclopedia of the Jesuits.

Tears

Cardinal Luis Antonio G. Tagle

The "seeds" of Pope Francis's theology of tears or weeping are contained in his homilies, meditations, and impromptu remarks. I witnessed the power of his words when he met the young people of the Philippines at the University of Santo Tomas in Manila on January 18, 2015. A boy and a girl, both street kids now living in a shelter, recounted their harrowing stories. The young girl, Glyzelle, addressed the pope in Filipino and burst into tears at the end of her speech. Pope Francis asked me what the girl had said and why she was crying. I translated her words for the pope: "Why does God allow the suffering of children?" Pope Francis departed from his prepared text and said, "Only when our hearts can ask this question and weep can we begin to understand. Let us learn to weep the way Glyzelle taught us today." This is just one of the many instances where Pope Francis teaches us what I will call the "Gospel of tears."

We do not want to lose the "naked and raw" beauty and power of Pope Francis's thought by forcing it into a systematic framework. But we can still indicate themes that recur when he speaks of tears and offer further reflection on them.

For Pope Francis the ability to shed tears and weep with and for others is a gift, a grace that we beg the Lord to grant. This might sound strange to a fun-seeking culture, jealously guarding its comfort zones. We don't search for occasions to lament. It would appear morbid to some people to even consider weeping as a blessing. But if it is a gift of God as Pope Francis claims, what good does it bring to us? From the pope's teachings

I discovered two wonderful blessings: tears deepen our relationship with Jesus, and they open paths for our mission of mercy and solidarity.

Meditating on Mary Magdalene's Easter proclamation to the apostles —"I have seen the Lord!"—Pope Francis says that tears of sorrow and uncertainty prepare us to see the Lord and testify to him. In many circumstances of life, tears lead us from obscurity to clarity (homily, April 2, 2013, and remarks in Manila, January 18, 2015). Many of us know by experience that at moments when we abandon our hearts and eyes to shed bitter tears, we also mysteriously abandon ourselves to God, enabling us to see God in a new light.

Seeing Jesus more clearly, we realize that he is also a man of tears, as the Scriptures narrate. Pope Francis points to Jesus knowing what it means to weep for a friend who died. He sheds tears of disappointment and fear (prayer vigil, May 5, 2016). I surmise that Jesus' tears enable him to see the human condition more clearly. We can say that his tears do not only affirm his being truly human, but also prepared him to see human beings as we truly are. By this clearer vision brought about by tears, Jesus becomes a compassionate brother to us rather than a harsh, non-feeling, and indifferent judge. Pierced with sorrow and tears, Jesus' heart turns to God in prayer, as the voice interceding for many sisters and brothers. This is the mystery we behold on the Cross, a mystery we could understand somehow by kneeling and weeping (homily, September 14, 2013). Tears prepare us to see Jesus. But I dare to add that Jesus' tears prepared him to see us as his brothers and sisters.

Pope Francis consistently associates Mother Mary with the tears of Jesus. She is always there, weeping for her son, weeping with him, and wiping our tears. Mary who accompanies Jesus walks with us too along the path of hope (prayer vigil, May 5, 2016). Pope Francis's reflections on the spirituality of tears draw our attention to great and strong women. I hear an invitation to see Jesus and our neighbours in a renewed way from the eyes of women washed by tears of hope.

We can gain new insights into the person and mission of Jesus by reflecting on his tears. And we can safely say that tears play a crucial role in our own Christian mission of mercy and solidarity. For Pope Francis tears prepare us to see neighbours—sisters and brothers—in other people by breaking the cycle of indifference and what I would call "cheap compassion." The Old Testament matriarch Rachel's refusal to be consoled at the death of her children expresses the depth of pain and bitterness in her tears. We can show sensitivity to the numerous Rachels of our time more by our tears of solidarity than with facile words and gestures (general audience, January 4, 2017). Words without tears cause more pain.

Looking at another biblical passage, Pope Francis notices the stark contrast between the tears of the sinful woman who welcomed Jesus and the cold civility of Simon the Pharisee who was supposed to be the real host (general audience, April 20, 2016). Failure to appreciate the tears of the vulnerable and broken-hearted unmasks our hypocrisy. Through our tears we witness to the need for humility, sincerity, and mercy in a world being destroyed by pride and pretensions. Hypocrites who hide their sins and weakness refuse to cry.

Like Jesus' tears, our tears serve as intercessory prayer for our brothers and sisters and for the whole world, especially the tears of pastors (address to Priests of Rome, March 6, 2014). But this is true not only for priests. While we cannot be faulted for weeping for ourselves, we must not lose the capacity to weep for others. In my years as a pastor, I have learned genuine prayer from parents who pray for their families often with tears, and once in a while with words.

I often wonder why I have not come across a reflection of Pope Francis on tears of joy. But perhaps there is no need for that. If tears enable us to see Jesus and testify to him, if tears make us see brothers and sisters in the spirit of solidarity, compassion, and humility, then tears manifest in a singular way the joy of the Gospel. People often ask me why smiles and genuine joy seem second nature to us Filipinos. I always say, "Because we have suffered and wept as a people, we know how to smile."

Cardinal Luis Antonio G. Tagle is the archbishop of Manila, Philippines. He also serves as president of Caritas Internationalis and president of the Catholic Biblical Federation.

Throwaway culture

Pat Farrell, OSF

When I think of Pope Francis's frequent mention of our "throwaway culture" I imagine him riding a bus, as he loved to do, in Buenos Aires. I can picture it: vendors getting on and off, peddling a wide variety of wares; the loud and lively interaction of groups of students; the noise and exhaust of a commuting world; the stale smell of alcohol and sweat; a few well-to-do people isolated by iPhones; the elderly, the animated, the preoccupied, the impoverished—in short, a cross-section of humanity momentarily sharing a crowded space. On the bus, what would have been the reverie of a thoughtful Jesuit not knowing he would one day be pope?

We will never know, but I think we can hear echoes of it now in his writings, with "why?" rising prominently from some reflective core. Why is there such unemployment, rendering vulnerable people so easily replaceable? Why are so many condemned to live on the material and existential margins? Why is there not more farsightedness in protecting the environment for future generations? Who pulls the strings that control the economic and financial policies of the globalized world? Why is there not more urgent concern for the health and welfare of the most impoverished among us? How can the church have more of an impact?

The questions Pope Francis articulates are hardly dispassionate. In an April 2014 audience with the Italian Movement for Life he urged: "We must also say, 'No to an economy of exclusion and inequality.' This economy kills. Human beings are themselves considered consumer goods to be used and then discarded. We have created a 'throwaway culture' which is now spreading. In this way life, too, is discarded."

On UN World Environment Day in 2013 he decried the world's waste of food, stating: "Throwing away food is like stealing from the table of the poor and the hungry." He exhorted large-scale conversion towards an "integral ecology" through "simple daily gestures which break with the logic of violence, exploitation, and selfishness," arguing that "in the end, a world of exacerbated consumption is at the same time a world which mistreats life in all its forms."

In a June 5, 2013, general audience in St. Peter's Square he lamented: "Men and women are sacrificed to the idols of money and consumption. That some homeless people freeze to death on the street, that is not news. On the other hand, a drop of 10 points in the stock markets of some cities is a tragedy. That is how people are thrown away. We, people, are thrown away, as if we were trash."

Hardly dispassionate, Pope Francis yet speaks from lucid social analysis, exposing systemic threads which link the destructive realities of domination, manipulation, and exploitation of people. He has named the mentality of profit at any price, with no concern for social exclusion or the destruction of nature. He has denounced a world economic and financial system lacking in ethics. He has called for a shift that would put the economy at the service of people rather than a situation in which human beings and nature are at the service of money. Time and again he has invited positive, redemptive change capable of releasing the human family from the bondage of individualism and the despondency it spawns. He has even asked world leaders gathered at the United Nations to redistribute wealth.

I hear in these pronouncements of Pope Francis the moral clarity of the Gospel spoken with genuine compassion. It is the human connection that makes his words all the more eloquent.

"We do not love concepts or ideas; we love people," Francis told participants of the Second World Meeting of Popular Movements in Bolivia in 2015. "Commitment, true commitment, is born of the love of men and women, of children and the elderly, of peoples and communities . . . of names and faces which fill our hearts. From those seeds of hope patiently sown in the forgotten fringes of our planet, from those seedlings of a tenderness which struggles to grow amid the shadows of exclusion, great trees will spring up, great groves of hope to give oxygen to our world."

Francis's life experience of proximity to those on the margins permeates these words he spoke in Bolivia:

When we look into the eyes of the suffering, when we see the faces of the endangered campesino, the poor labourer, the downtrodden native, the homeless family, the persecuted migrant, the unemployed young person, the exploited child, the mother who lost her child in a shootout because the barrio was occupied by drug dealers, the father who lost his daughter to enslavement. . . . when we think of all those names and faces, our hearts break because of so much sorrow and pain. And we are deeply moved. . . . We are moved because "we have seen and heard" not a cold statistic but the pain of a suffering humanity, our own pain, our own flesh. This is something quite different than abstract theorizing or eloquent indignation. It moves us; it makes us attentive to others in an effort to move forward together. That emotion which turns into community action is not something which can be understood by reason alone: it has a surplus of meaning which only peoples understand, and it gives a special feel to genuine popular movements.

I know from experience that literally rubbing shoulders on a crowded bus creates embodied memory. The illusion of separation is shattered when body parts collide. That physical knowing endures. We have a pope whose thighs have pressed against those of weary seat companions. Distance from human suffering is just not part of who he is. May it become impossible for all of us!

Sr. Pat Farrell is a member of the Sisters of St. Francis of Dubuque, Iowa. She served as the president of the Leadership Conference of Women Religious in 2011–12 and has spent many years living and working in Chile, El Salvador, and Honduras.

Women

Astrid Lobo Gajiwala

The jury is still out on Pope Francis's position on women. "Is he pro-woman?" is a question left hanging in the air.

I like to believe that he is getting there. Not because he has made any sweeping changes to benefit women, but because his internal compass seems to be pointing in the right direction. He is sensitive towards women's subordination both in the church and in the world, and he is emphatic in his denouncement of it. In the very first year of his pontificate when addressing the Pontifical Council for the Laity at their symposium on *Mulieris Dignitatem* he shared: "I suffer . . . when I see in the church or in some ecclesial organizations . . . that women's role of service slips into a role of servitude." Three years later while speaking to the International Union of Superiors General he went a step further. "When you Superiors are asked for something that is more servitude than service," he advised them, "have the courage to say 'no.'"

In *Amoris Laetitia*, Francis tackles head-on the "headship" of the man in the family. He rejects "every form of sexual submission"—including interpretations that misuse Paul's exhortation to women to be subject to their husbands (Eph 5:22)—and goes so far as to call out marital rape (AL 154). I can only hope Catholics here in India and their pastors are listening. We are one of the few countries in the world that has resisted criminalizing marital rape due to a culture that continues to believe that if men are deprived of their marital "rights" and women are given the power to say "no" to their "lord and master," it could destroy the institution of marriage.

At a more proactive level, Pope Francis's call two years ago for "a more widespread and incisive female presence in the community" set the church abuzz. He made this statement during an address to members of the Pontifical Council for Culture in February 2015 and qualified it by saying that we would then see "many women involved in pastoral responsibilities, in the accompaniment of people, families and groups, as well as in theological reflection." He did not mention decision-making. In the same speech, though, he made a strong plea for the promotion of women in the public sphere, in "places where the most important decisions are taken." This ambiguity left the door open for much speculation about what he meant and how he proposed to walk the talk. One lost opportunity was the 2015 Synod on the Family, however, which appointed thirty women as auditors but gave none of them the right to vote. Other debates have centred on what Francis meant when he told Jesuit Fr. Antonio Spadaro in a 2013 interview that the church has to "work harder to develop a profound theology of women." Was this to be seen as opposed to a theology of men? Did it imply that the existing theology was a theology of men? Did he perhaps mean a theology *by* women?

Pope Francis's take on feminism too has been confusing. In his 2016 meeting with the International Union of Superiors General, he named feminism as one of two "temptations . . . against which we must guard," because falling into feminism "would reduce a woman's importance." And yet, at a weekly general audience in April 2015 he had reflected on the current decline in marriages and absolved the women's rights movement of blame, calling attempts to fault women's emancipation a form of "chauvinism" that seeks to "control the woman." At the same audience he further exhorted the crowds to demand the "radical equality" that Christianity emphasizes between husbands and wives—something he strongly reinforces in *Amoris Laetitia*, seeing in "the women's movement the working of the Spirit for a clearer recognition of the dignity and rights of women" (AL 54). Francis's lexicon on women now includes words like "reciprocity" (AL 54) and concepts like "equal compensation for equal work" (general audience, April 29, 2015), and "freedom of choice" (AL 33)—including the need to ensure that women are not "left alone to carry the burden of deciding between the family and an effective presence" in public and ecclesial life (address to Pontifical Council for Culture, February 7, 2015). It makes one wonder: does he even realize that these theories that have now entered the mainstream of just practices have their origins in feminism? Or that they do not stand alone but are interlinked with all that affects women's rights and interests?

No matter his understanding, his advocacy on behalf of women has women cheering until they come up against his wall of "complementarity of the sexes." It is a notion that surfaces repeatedly in Francis's teachings, no doubt taking its cue from Pope John Paul II's 1988 apostolic letter *Mulieris Dignitatem*. However, as Creighton University theologians Michael Lawler and Todd Salzman pointed out in a May 2015 article for *National Catholic Reporter*, Francis uses the term "complementarity" in a different way than John Paul. While John Paul used the term in a rigid and universal, classicist way, "defining it to reflect traditional and culturally determined gender roles grounded in the physiological distinction between male and female," Francis's speech reflects a historically conscious view that is "dynamic, evolving, changing and particular."

In his speech to a 2014 Vatican colloquium on "The Complementarity of Man and Woman in Marriage," Francis argued that "complementarity will take many forms as each man and woman brings his or her distinctive contributions to their marriage and to the formation of their children—his or her personal richness, personal charisma." Thus, while Francis never ceases to promote motherhood he simultaneously encourages wider roles for women and recognizes the necessity for changes in social and ecclesial systems to make this possible. In *Amoris Laetitia* he gives gender stereotypes short shrift, stating that "masculinity and femininity are not rigid categories" and that art and dance are expressions of being "masculine" as much as the exercise of leadership is an expression of being "feminine." He also advocates shared household chores and childcare (AL 286).

Unfortunately, the theological anthropology that underpins Francis's complementarity does not stop with social questions. It extends to the ordination of women. On more than one occasion Pope Francis has made definitive statements supporting his predecessors' ban on the ordination of women. Citing John Paul II's 1994 apostolic letter *Ordinatio Sacerdotalis*, Francis reasons that ordaining women is not possible because Jesus chose only men as his apostles, and since a priest "acts in the person of Christ," a priest must be male. He buttresses this traditional argument with the contention that ordaining women would end up clericalizing them. He has been vociferous in his protests against the "disease" of clericalism, but something does not ring quite true when one reads his March 2017 interview with the German weekly *Die Zeit*. Francis admits that due to the lack of vocations "in many communities at the moment, committed women are preserving Sunday as a day of worship by holding services of the Word. But a church without the Eucharist has no strength." His solution, however, is not to consider the ordination of the women who are already ministering in parishes, but to discuss the ordination of "proven married men," known in Latin as *viri probati*. For all his profession of equality of the sexes, Francis seems convinced that God cannot be as sacramentally present through the body of a woman priest as God can be in the body of a male priest. It would appear too that the fears he harbours of women being sucked into clericalism do not apply to married men.

So where does that leave the women, given that governance in the church is linked with ordination? Dependent on Francis. When the superiors of women religious asked Pope Francis in 2016 to constitute an official commission to study the question of a permanent diaconate for women, he immediately agreed and followed through later with the creation of a twelve-member commission that includes noted academic Phyllis Zagano, whose advocacy for women deacons is well known. Francis has cautioned, though, that this is not opening a door, but is merely to throw light on the subject. So how it will end is anyone's guess.

On the other hand, Pope Francis's strong push for the inclusion of women in different Vatican offices is already beginning to bear fruit. When the women religious requested to be included in the plenary assembly of the Congregation for the Institutes of Consecrated Life and Societies of Apostolic Life, he agreed with alacrity. In 2014 he approved the appointment of Sr. Mary Melone as the first woman rector of Rome's Pontifical University Antonianum. The International Theological Commission currently has an all-time high of five women theologians out of thirty members, and Francis has expressed the desire to see their numbers increase. The formerly all-male Pontifical Council for Culture now has a thirty-seven-member Women's Consultation Group that brings the voices of women to "stimulate the reflection" of the council's members on universal issues.

Despite these positive signs, however, Pope Francis continues to keep leadership positions in the dicasteries out of bounds for women. He believes that appointing women as heads of Vatican offices would promote a "functionalism" of women's roles in the Catholic Church. It is no surprise therefore, that he appointed a priest as secretary of the new Dicastery for Laity, Family and Life, which became effective in 2016, even though the office's statutes make provision for the appointment of a lay person. However, five months later in what seems to be a balancing move, he appointed two married women as undersecretaries: Linda Ghisoni, a seasoned canon lawyer and judge, for the section on laity; and Gabriella Gambino, a bioethics professor, for the section on life.

With all his contradictions, his occasionally misplaced, if well-intentioned humour, and his sometimes off-colour remarks about women that expose the benevolent patriarchy from which he operates, Pope Francis has done more to empower women in the church than any pontiff before him. It cannot be easy walking the tight rope between the official teachings of the church with their patriarchal underpinnings and the truth he perceives in the lives of the women around him, but one thing Francis is not short of is the courage to act on his convictions. Already his interpretation and application of doctrine have attracted public censure, even from his fellow bishops, but this has not deterred him. At the other end, many criticize him for his refusal to change church teaching. His reasoning, however, is clear. In a March 2014 interview with Italy's *Corriere della Sera*, he explained: "The question is not that of changing the doctrine, but to go deep and to ensure that pastoral care takes into account situations and what is possible for people." It is a position that is reminiscent of Jesus' radical understanding of the law (Matt 5:1-11, 17) and displays a rootedness in the experience of people, not in abstract academics. But it is also a strategy to not attract attention and quietly lay the groundwork for future change.

It would seem that much of Pope Francis's understanding of women's situation is intuitive, not drawn from any principles or ideology, and that perhaps is why he is unable to see the threads of patriarchy and sexism that run through so much of church teaching. It would also account for the contradictions and inconsistencies in his stand. At the same time, it appears that sometimes he simply likes to stir the pot, to generate a conversation in the church around an issue he considers important in the hope of giving it necessary attention. Women find the flavours of his meals sometimes sweet, sometimes bitter, but tasty enough to whet their appetite and ask for more.

Astrid Lobo Gajiwala has a PhD in medicine and postgraduate diplomas in tissue banking, bioethics, and theology. She is a resource person for the Federation of Asian Bishops' Conference and the Catholic Bishops' Conference of India, and a consultor for the Indian bishops' Commission for Women. She was a member of the drafting committee for the Indian bishops' Gender Policy of the Catholic Church of India *and contributed to their* Guidelines to Deal with Sexual Harrassment at the Workplace.

Worldliness

Mollie Wilson O'Reilly

Christians, Pope Francis says, are on a mission "to light a fire in the heart of this world." That's the striking image he uses near the end of his first major written work, *Evangelii Gaudium*, in which he calls Catholics to spread the Gospel in the modern world by becoming "men and women of the people." He echoes it at the end of his urgent encyclical *Laudato Si'*. And how do we reach "the heart of this world"? It starts with realizing we're not already there.

When Jorge Bergoglio was introduced as Pope Francis from the balcony of St. Peter's Basilica in 2013, he joked that his brother cardinals had gone "to the ends of the world" to find a new bishop for the Diocese of Rome. Of course, as pope, that bishop leads the worldwide church—and even so, the selection of a Jesuit from Argentina was a shock. Bergoglio wasn't on anybody's short list. He seemed to have come out of nowhere.

As Pope Francis, he has reminded us again and again that getting stuck in this way of seeing the world, which accepts the power structures in place as the God-given order of things, prevents us from fulfilling God's purpose. It may be comfortable to presume that the rich and powerful nations are the most important (at least for those of us who come from those nations). We may be content to allow the people on the margins—at the ends of the world, as it were—to remain marginalized. But if we truly want to spread the Gospel, Francis explains in *Evangelii Gaudium*, we must be willing to go beyond the boundaries that make us feel secure. And protecting the earth, he writes in *Laudato Si'*, requires facing up to the disproportionate effects the actions of wealthy nations have on developing ones and acknowledging that environmental injustice is the result of our own choices and not an expression of God's mysterious will. We are all connected, and our "interdependence obliges us to think of *one world with a common plan*" (LS 164).

In short, to follow Christ we must learn to see and love the world as he does. That is what will make it possible to light that fire in the heart of the world: when we stop seeing ourselves as set apart from or more important than the other people and other creatures with whom we share the earth. The pope writes at length in *Evangelii Gaudium* about a condition he calls "spiritual worldliness," which "consists in seeking not the Lord's glory but human glory and personal well-being." A spiritually worldly person is content to feel superior to others, rather than reaching out in humble fellowship. The antidote to this "tremendous corruption disguised as a good" is "making the church constantly go out from herself" to spread the Gospel. "As believers," Francis writes in *Laudato Si'*, "we do not look at the world from without but from within, conscious of the bonds with which the Father has linked us to all beings" (LS 220). When we see the world this way, as a "web of relationships," we also recognize that the centre of that web is not us: not Americans, or Westerners, or Catholics, or Christians, or even humans, but the triune God—Father, Son, and Spirit. "The ultimate purpose of other creatures is not to be found in us," Francis writes. "Rather, all creatures are moving forward with us and through us towards a common point of arrival, which is God" (LS 83).

Over and over, in his writing and speeches and in his actions, Francis shows how the church can live his vision of inclusivity. He redirects our attention to the margins when he celebrates Holy Thursday Mass in prison and includes non-Christians in the footwashing rite, and when he promotes bishops from underrepresented parts of the globe, rather than awarding important titles only to already prominent dioceses. And, recalling his days as "the bishop of the slums" in Buenos Aires, Francis constantly reminds the powerful to regard the poor and marginalized not just as objects of our charity but as people whose communities and insights deserve our respect. He doesn't just speak to the marginalized, he amplifies their voices for all to hear. In *Laudato Si'* he makes a point of discussing the impact of climate change and uneven global development on indigenous peoples; he nods to the special insights of the elderly in assessing the damage already done to the planet; and he quotes from bishops' conferences around the world to make his point that the need for a global response is already being felt in many parts of the earth.

Francis has been known to use the word "world" in a negative sense. He calls Satan "the prince of this world" and cautions against choosing the satisfactions that the world can give over the peace Jesus offers us. A "worldly" church, he said in his April 30, 2013, homily in Domus Sanctae Marthae, "is a weak church, a defeated church, unable to transmit the Gospel." But Francis more often describes the world as a gift, created by, loved by and infused with the presence of God. "It is true that in our dealings with the world, we are told to give reasons for our hope," he says in *Evangelii Gaudium*, "but not as an enemy who critiques and condemns" (EG 271). For Francis, the world is not to be feared or held at arm's length, but embraced—provided we remember that it is God's kingdom and not ours. "Through our worship of God, we are invited to embrace the world on a different plane," he writes in *Laudato Si'*. God "has united himself definitively to our earth," and the sacraments use the material of creation—water, wheat, oil, wine—to make God's presence visible. In the Eucharist, Christ "comes not from above, but from within, he comes that we might find him in this world of ours" (LS 236).

As refreshing and joyful as it can be, Francis's message is not always a comfortable one, because embracing it requires conversion—especially for those of us in positions of privilege. We have to reorient ourselves. We have to let go of comfortable illusions and self-centred "worldliness." We have to commit to real companionship with our fellow creatures if we want to light that fire Francis talks about in *Evangelii Gaudium*. The path of conversion may be painful. But it will lead us out of ourselves to the true "heart of this world"—and, as Francis writes in *Laudato Si'*, "In the heart of this world, the Lord of Life, who loves us so much, is always present" (LS 245).

Mollie Wilson O'Reilly is an editor-at-large and columnist for Commonweal *magazine. She lives in Bronxville, New York, with her husband and four young sons.*

Youth

Jordan Denari Duffner

In the mid-1950s, a young high-schooler studying chemistry quietly entered the Basilica of St. Joseph in Buenos Aires. Making the sign of the cross, he walked under the sanctuary's gilded arches and slipped into a confessional to receive the sacrament of reconciliation. The moment of prayer changed Jorge Bergoglio's life.

"After confession I felt that something had changed. I was no longer the same person. I had really heard a voice, a call: I felt that I had to become a priest," he recounted in Elisabetta Piqué's 2013 biography of him, *Life and Revolution*, many decades later after being elected pope. The teenage Jorge had felt inclinations towards the priesthood before, and those who knew him could see that even as a young person he was gifted at ministering to the needs of others and teaching about the Catholic faith. But that "meeting" with Jesus in the confessional was a pivotal and definitive moment, one that set him on his course to be a Jesuit priest who sought to serve those on the peripheries. His calling in the Basilica of St. Joseph has remained so central to his own self-understanding and ministry as a priest that he chose his episcopal motto—"seeing him with the eyes of mercy and choosing him"—in memory of feeling God's call to him as a young person.

For Pope Francis, this call from God—which came to him in his youth—clearly shapes his approach to youth today. When he addresses young people, he very frequently talks about vocation, trying to guide them to an encounter with the Lord like the one he had as a boy. In many

Catholic contexts, "vocation" is most often used in reference to callings to the priesthood, religious life, or marriage. But Pope Francis recognizes that vocations are broader and, at the same time, *deeper* than that. For Francis, every vocation is born of an encounter with Jesus, who calls us to be more deeply ourselves, and who challenges us to give ourselves over to the service of others (message for 54th World Day of Prayer for Vocations, November 27, 2016). These vocations are unique to each person and can be manifested in various ways.

I received my call at the same age Pope Francis did, seventeen. On a Sunday afternoon in the spring of 2008, I opened my inbox to find an email that had circulated among many of my friends' parents in my Catholic parish, and contained a rambling message that warned of the danger posed by another religious community: Muslims. The email cast Muslims as "our enemy," effectively pinning the violence of a few on an entire faith group.

A teenager growing up in the Midwest, I didn't know many people who were Muslim—just a few classmates at my Jesuit high school. But the apparent hostility my fellow Catholics felt towards Muslims deeply unsettled me. My mother consoled and encouraged me. "That's why you have to write," she said.

Throughout childhood I had always desired to be a writer, but in that moment I learned what that passion was for: helping my own Catholic community better understand the Muslims of whom they were so fearful. That email, and my mother's encouragement, turned out to be a key vocational moment through which I began to understand the challenge to which God was calling me. And I didn't wait until I was an adult to begin living it out. While still a college student, I published articles about my experiences of interreligious dialogue with Muslim students at my university, and I attempted to shed light on manifestations of anti-Muslim prejudice. Later, my mother told me: "What I told you after you received that email—those words didn't come from me; they were from the Holy Spirit."

I think Pope Francis would be proud of the way my mother helped foster my vocation in my youth. During his papacy, Pope Francis has set as one of his priorities for the church helping young people to recognize their own calling from God. At World Youth Days and other events, the pope speaks to youth about the importance of developing a friendship with Jesus, of opening oneself to an encounter with God. He frequently issues public prayers, sometimes via tweet or viral video, asking God that young people understand and respond to Jesus' unique mission for them. In 2017, the Vatican released an online survey to better understand the needs and viewpoints of young adults, in preparation for the 2018 Synod of Bishops, which Pope Francis said will be dedicated to "young people, faith and vocational discernment."

Though he doesn't mention it explicitly, Ignatian spirituality permeates the vocabulary and substance of Pope Francis's advice to youth, as evidenced by his frequent use of the word "discernment." In the spirituality of the Jesuits, the order of priests, deacons, and brothers to which Pope Francis belongs, discernment is the ongoing, prayerful process of understanding God's desires for us and learning how to respond to those desires in the way we live. Pope Francis encourages youth to engage in discernment through reading the Bible and seeking advice from elders, especially grandparents. (Like me, Jorge was also supported in his vocational call by a family matriarch—his grandmother—who, Piqué writes, told him: "Well, if God calls you, so be it!")

Francis also recommends that young people commit to a "daily examination of conscience," a staple prayer in the Ignatian tradition that consists of looking back over one's day and noticing one's emotions and desires. In Ignatian spirituality, those deepest desires are important to pay attention to because they are also God's desires—God's dreams—for us.

Pope Francis has pointed to St. Joseph, the patron of the basilica where he first felt called, as an example for young people of what it means to allow God's dreams for us to become our own. Joseph, too, was a young person when God called him in a dream to wed Mary, Francis said in a homily for the feast of St. Joseph in May 2017. Joseph teaches us that "when we dream great things, beautiful things," we "draw near to the dream of God, the things God dreams about us."

But as the example of Joseph also illustrates, living out those dreams comes with risks and challenges, and it requires the taking on of "difficult tasks." It wasn't easy for Joseph to take on the responsibility of raising Jesus as his own. God demands "real courage," Francis told young people at World Youth Day in Poland in 2016, because responding to our vocation often means eschewing society's expectations and focusing on God's countercultural call.

Even amid the hardships, Pope Francis says, young people should feel encouraged and energized by the fact that the world deeply needs young people. Just like my mother said when I received that troubling email as a high-schooler, Pope Francis assures young people that they can begin living their vocation now, not down the road when they are older. With his own experience ever in mind, Francis recognizes that it is not despite their youth but because of it that young people have something valuable to offer.

Now, almost a decade since my own vocational turning point, I'm nearing the end of my young adult years. But, in the pope and in my mother, I have examples of how to support the next generation of youth in their journey to discover their own calls from God. And I echo Pope Francis's brief prayer for youth, which he aptly shared in a May 1, 2017, tweet: "May St. Joseph give young people the ability to dream, to take risks for big tasks, the things that God dreams for us."

Jordan Denari Duffner is the author of Finding Jesus among Muslims: How Loving Islam Makes Me a Better Catholic *(Liturgical Press). An associate with Georgetown University's Bridge Initiative, where she has also worked as a research fellow studying Islamophobia, Jordan is now pursuing a PhD in theological and religious studies, also at Georgetown. A former Fulbright researcher in Amman, Jordan, she has written for numerous publications about Muslim–Christian dialogue.*

Acknowledgments

Pope Francis famously called his 2013 encyclical letter *Lumen Fidei* "a work of four hands," giving credit to Pope Benedict XVI's initial drafting of the document before his resignation of the papacy. The volume before you is the work of hundreds of hands. Words cannot adequately convey our gratitude to everyone involved.

First, to our contributors: thank you each for your unending graciousness in taking part in this endeavour, and for putting up with email after email of reminders of looming deadlines. We think readers will agree that your insights give Pope Francis's words new depth and definition.

Barry Hudock, a publisher at Liturgical Press, first approached us in December 2016 about putting together some essays about the way Pope Francis talks, inspired by the 2015 Italian volume *Il Vocabolario di Papa Francesco*, which was edited by Antonio Carriero and published by Elledici. We thank Elledici for their cooperation and their blessing on this project and Barry for his tenacity, insight, and persistence, which were simply essential to the creation of this book. Others at Liturgical Press were likewise important, including Michelle Verkuilen, whose work in promoting the volume included learning some HTML to make the website announcement shine, and J. Andrew Edwards, who handled the initial editing of the full manuscript.

Many people were extraordinarily helpful in connecting us with possible contributors. In this regard, we thank Archbishop Roberto González Nieves, Anglican Archbishop David Moxon, Orthodox Fr. John Chryssavgis, Michael Sean Winters, and Brenda Nettles Riojas.

We especially want to thank the bosses at our day jobs: Greg Erlandson, director and editor-in-chief of Catholic News Service; and Dennis Coday, editor-in-chief of *National Catholic Reporter*. We are most grateful for your understanding as we took part in a time-intensive project outside the normal scope of our individual duties.

Both of the editors are supported in their daily lives by a wide range of people close to their hearts. Cindy thanks especially her sister and best friend Cheryl, who is always supportive, generous, and encouraging. Joshua thanks his wife Kate, who is a source of solace, creativity, and boundless energy.

We reserve our biggest thanks, of course, for Pope Francis, whose words and actions since his election to the papacy on March 13, 2013, have inspired, sparked the imagination, and left what we might call more than adequate room for further reflection.

From Rome
September 2017